BRAZILIANS IN DIALOGUE BETWEEN THE UNIVERSITY AND THE PRISON

Karina Biondi (Ed)

BRAZILIANS IN DIALOGUE BETWEEN THE UNIVERSITY AND THE PRISON

The Incarceration Nations Network Collection

Collection Editor
Baz Dreisinger

LPp

First published in 2025 by Lived Places Publishing

British Library Cataloguing in Publication Data
A CIP record for this book is available from the British Library.

ISBN: 9781917503129 (pbk)
ISBN: 9781917503143 (ePDF)
ISBN: 9781917503136 (ePUB)

The right of Karina Biondi to be identified as the Author of this work has been asserted by them in accordance with the Copyright, Design and Patents Act 1988.

Cover design by Fiachra McCarthy
Book design by Rachel Trolove of Twin Trail Design
Typeset by Newgen Publishing, UK

Lived Places Publishing
P.O. Box 1845
47 Echo Avenue
Miller Place, NY 11764

www.livedplacespublishing.com

Abstract

This book is the result of a project based in Brazil that offered training to former incarcerated persons, enabling them to systematize their knowledge about prison. The idea is that no one is better suited than those who have lived the prison experience to speak about it and produce knowledge on crime and punishment. The chapters gathered in this book offer a small sample of the richness of the reflections carried out during the project. Its contribution to the field of studies on crime and incarceration demonstrates the importance of investing in the intellectual development of individuals who are already experts in prison life.

Key words

Prisons; education; incarceration; Brazil; desistance; Convict Criminology

Presentation

Dr Fernando Mendonça[1]

First, I would like to express my gratitude to Professor Karina Biondi for the invitation to present this book. It helps me relive a little of my time in the early 2000s as an assistant judge at the 1st Criminal Enforcement Court in Maranhão, Brazil, and an unfulfilled dream of creating a storytelling project with people in prison. This book takes me back to that period, with ideals that were realized and others that were not.

The functions of the criminal enforcement judge are completely different from those of the criminal action judge, who is responsible for hearing criminal cases. While the former judges the citizen who committed the crime, convicting or acquitting them, the latter has the main obligation to carry out the determinations contained in the sentence handed down. In my view, the second primary role of the enforcement judge is to believe in the social reintegration of the convicted person and to do everything possible to achieve this objective.

Brazil and Latin America serve as poor examples when it comes to arresting and imprisoning individuals. When they make arrests, they often do so in a disastrous manner. Generally, they arrest people in flagrante delicto with minimal evidence, as poor or Black individuals do not have the best lawyers to secure their freedom. Technical investigations, in turn, are inefficient in terms of equipment and personnel. Furthermore, the culture of criminalizing poverty is a natural consequence of the abject history of colonization and slavery.

The prison system has always segregated, mixed, and made invisible those who commit any crime. Those who have gone through this experience have been marked by the scourges of a prison system that the Brazilian Supreme Federal Court has deemed an "unconstitutional state of affairs."

The stigma of imprisonment remains forever in the soul of the convicted person and often in their body. For a long time, this mark permeates their social relationships. Reintegration into society takes time and requires a superhuman effort from the individual, especially when they are young. Resilience and persistence are key concepts, but they are not enough. The State must advance public policies on education, health, employment, and income to prevent crime, in addition to providing internal training and professional studies, so that the ex-prisoner can, upon leaving prison, no longer find "chains" as a welcome and shelter.

The need to overcome the scars of incarceration in an exclusionary, oppressive, and discriminatory society does not contribute to the social harmony and peace that the law desires. On the contrary, contributing to personal transformation is a collective duty of society. It is up to those who govern and those who are governed to engage in building a world without profound inequalities and injustices, investing massively in universal and quality education. This was the case in Europe after centuries of class conflicts and in the "Asian Tigers" after the Second World War. This was a social demand from everyone for everyone, without distinction.

Freedom and guarantees of formal, existential, and fundamental rights alone are not enough. Crime deserves punishment, that's true. But what crime? What punishment? Punishments at will for those born into slavery? For those who don't have the money to pay for a good lawyer?

I have been a big fan of the project of Convict Criminology[2] since its beginning. I met Sacha at a conference in Goiânia around 2015, and I was fascinated by his project at the University of Westminster. A few years later, a mutual friend introduced me to Professor Karina Biondi, accompanied by Professor Sacha Darke, at my Judicial Unit (2nd Criminal Enforcement Court).

It was a great pleasure to participate in the opening of the Criminology Course offered in Maranhão (see more details in the introduction to this book) and to spend some time with students who have left the prison system in Maranhão. The door to knowledge and experience is opening, and it is the key to the true liberation of these individuals. At first, it will be slow, but over time, the expansion of knowledge and new experiences will reveal the true dimension of the human being that each person carries within themselves.

No one improves or transforms outside of their family, community, or society. The experience of studying, of good relationships, and of their continuity are the richest experiences that any citizen should have as a basic right. This can only be achieved in an environment that, in the good fight for social and economic rights, transforms itself into an inclusive, supportive, and cooperative society.

"My family, who I have made cry so many times, is proud of the person I am today," wrote Alex Saraiva in this book. On his behalf, I salute the authors of the collection, especially those who carry the stigma of prison in their souls and bodies. Their efforts to overcome the scars of incarceration and to be a source of pride for their families are expressed in the texts they wrote for this book.

Before concluding, I must thank the CIAPIS/SEAP management for their partnership. It was worth it!

Contents

Foreword

The transformative potential that education offers to prisoners and ex-prisoners is vast and, for some, life-changing. Higher education, in particular, has the potential to open up a range of prosocial opportunities and life options that would otherwise be unavailable to many who have lost their freedom. For those incarcerated, education is also critical in helping many survive. After prison, education can be used as currency to negotiate the stigma typically experienced by ex-prisoners in the "mainstream world."

At the same time, the perspectives of prisoners and ex-prisoners are virtually absent from the discipline of criminology. Academics—most from privileged backgrounds—conduct their research on, not with, prisoners and ex-prisoners, who are rarely given the space to interpret and articulate their own voices. This is the starting point for Convict Criminology, a scholarly movement led by ex-prisoners and a critical perspective that I draw on throughout my research, engagement, and writing on prison. Convict Criminology aims to develop insider approaches to crime and justice through the work of prisoners and ex-prisoners who are studying in higher education, and the work of established academics who have served prison sentences in the past. It privileges their knowledge and understanding and, in doing so, provides an alternative critical analysis grounded in lived experience. The engagement of prisoners and ex-prisoners in higher education is equally significant in this regard.

The first Convict Criminology group was formally established in the United States in the 1990s, at a time when the university and prison sectors were expanding, and more people began to study criminology after prison. Many of these former students complained that the theories and representations of crime and prison that they read in criminology texts did not reflect their personal experiences. That is, except for the work of John Irwin, who revolutionized sociological theory about prison life in the 1960s and 1970s when, with his PhD advisor, Donald Cressey, he challenged the assumption that American prisons are isolated from the outside world and that incarcerated persons' cultures are distinct from those found in the wider community. John Irwin was only the second American criminologist to come out as a former prisoner. The first, Frank Tannenbaum, was famous for his pioneering work on labeling theory in the 1930s, but not for his work on prisons. Today, there are dozens of American criminologists who have served time in prison.

Like our American colleagues who laid the foundations of Convict Criminology, our vision at the University of Westminster is to develop prison research that is authentically informed by lived experience. However, there are too few ex-prisoners, let alone university professors, in British academia to achieve this. That's why we decided to bring higher education in-house.

Since 2012, Dr Andreas (Andy) Aresti and I have been running a study group in Convict Criminology at the University of Westminster. Andy served a prison sentence in the 1990s. We have also started four initiatives to support current prisoners through higher education since 2014: an academic mentoring scheme, which has so far supported around 50 incarcerated students, and education programmes at Pentonville, Grendon, and Coldingley prisons in England. The Pentonville programme was validated as an undergraduate criminology module in 2018. The Coldingley and Grendon programmes were validated into our Global Criminology MSc programme in 2022. Eligible prison and university students will now receive university credits for each of these programmes. Our study group now includes a second ex-prisoner and former prison officer criminology lecturer, Sinem Bozkurt, and two PhD students, both of whom we taught for the first time at Coldingley. It also includes a prison officer PhD student we met at Pentonville. A graduate from Coldingley and another from HMP Grendon have also been accepted into places to start our MA Global Criminology programme, of which I am Director.

Our prison-based programmes involve students from the University of Westminster studying and publishing in criminology alongside prisoners who are also studying for degrees in social sciences. In 2018, we were invited to edit a special issue of the *Journal of Prisoners on Prisons* celebrating the 20th anniversary of Convict Criminology. The issue included articles written by members of the study groups at Grendon and Coldingley. In June 2023, we organised the first Convict Criminology symposium on higher education in the three prisons. A fourth day was held at the university and included presentations by prisoners in Brazil via videoconference. As far as we know, it was also the first international academic symposium on prison to take place inside a prison. Karina Biondi and Francisco Lopes de Magalhães Filho (Chicão) presented the work of Outra Visão on each day of the symposium. Chicão also presented a paper on the lack of healthcare in São Paulo prisons. All of the presentations will later be published in a collection of collaborative writings between university students and prisoners.

It was in this context that it was an honor to receive the invitation from Professor Karina Biondi to write the preface to *Another Vision: Dialogues between University and Prison*. Andy Aresti and I participated in the first Outra Visão program at the State University of Maranhão (UEMA), at APAC in São Luís, in 2019, and we returned with our students in April of this year to participate in the current program held at the university, where we met some of the formerly incarcerated students who wrote articles for this groundbreaking book. With an emphasis on collaborative teaching and learning about crime and punishment, Outra Visão is certainly the first and only education program based on the Convict Criminology in Latin America, and *Diálogos entre a Universidade e a Prisão* is the first book on the Convict Criminology in Latin America. Similar to our Westminster Convict Criminology programmes, *Another Vision* is grounded in Paulo Freire's emancipatory pedagogy and his insistence on co-produced knowledge and horizontal study, in this case between people with and without lived experience of prison. Simply put, Outra Visão would not be a project on the Convict Criminology without Chicão playing a central role alongside Karina in teaching. Nor, in my opinion, would a project on Convict Criminology be as good without the participation of university students as well as prisoners and ex-prisoners.

Some of our colleagues in the US and UK argue that those who have never been arrested do not have the knowledge needed to identify themselves as convicted criminologists. For Andy Aresti and me, it is an epistemological fallacy to make such a rigid distinction between those who have been to prison, whether long or short, and those who have not. Furthermore, Convict Criminology is concerned with challenging existing hierarchies of knowledge, not creating new ones. Some Westminster and UEMA students have spent dozens, if not hundreds, of hours studying and co-producing criminological knowledge with prisoners and ex-prisoners. And some of our most dedicated students—from inside and outside prisons—also share similar life experiences. The same cannot be said for most of its professors, many of whom still claim to be experts on an institution they have rarely visited and on people whose lives are a distant reality from their own.

Dr Sacha Darke,

Professor of Criminology, University of Westminster,

4 August 2023

Introduction

Karina Biondi[3]

In 2019, I was invited by my colleague Sacha Darke from the University of Westminster to develop a project at APAC, a prison that follows an alternative model in which incarcerated persons hold the keys to their own prison. The project would be modeled on *Making Links*, coordinated by him and Andreas Aresti in the United Kingdom. In this project, they offer criminology classes inside prisons for incarcerated persons, as well as for students enrolled at their university. In order to avoid imposing a hierarchy among the students, they are called "students on the inside" and "students on the outside," with the "students on the outside" helping the "students on the inside" in carrying out the proposed activities.

> Sacha and Andreas's project is part of an international movement called "Convict Criminology" (better described in the preface and chapter written by Walsh, Ammerer, and Bonnick in this book). According to this movement, no one is better suited than people who have lived the prison experience up close or in their own skin to talk about it, analyze the prison issue, and ultimately produce knowledge about crime and punishment. The idea is to encourage and promote the entry of these people into academic production on the subject. In this scheme, it is important for a former prisoner to work on the project, both to help in the classes and to show the incarcerated

persons that entry into academic life is, in fact, possible. In the English project, this role is filled by Andreas Aresti, a former prisoner and currently a professor of criminology at the University of Westminster.

In England, the project has already supported the training of graduates, master's, and doctoral students. Other initiatives in other countries (such as the United States, Argentina, and Mexico) have also shown very good results. However, its implementation in Brazil, specifically in Maranhão, posed some challenges and required adjustments to the original project. The main challenge was adapting the English project to a context in which a large part of the prison population has barely completed elementary school and where there are significant bureaucratic difficulties in bringing education to prisons.

Therefore, in order to bring the project to Brazil, specifically to Maranhão, I assessed that adaptations would be necessary. In 2019, we began visiting APAC to get to know the incarcerated persons and their profiles better. One characteristic of APAC is the small number of incarcerated persons, so it was possible to speak to all those in the closed regime. Among them, there were individuals who already had higher education, but also those who could barely sign their names. Francisco, a former incarcerated person of the Brazilian prison system who worked on the project from the beginning (in line with the English project that inspired us), warned us that selecting only a few incarcerated persons for the courses we intended to offer would introduce a new form of exclusion for people who had already suffered several exclusion processes throughout their lives. "We will not leave any little brother out, no," he said at the time.

This observation was fundamental for the reflections that were triggered throughout the project, as well as for the format it took. In order to "not leave any little brother out," we accepted people without any educational prerequisites. The only condition to participate in the project was to have been imprisoned. After all, we consider, in line with the Convict Criminology (Aresti et al., 2023; Darke and Aresti, 2016; Earle, 2016; Ross and Vianello, 2021; Ross and Copes, 2022) and certain anthropological perspectives (Latour, 2005; Strathern, 1988), that people who live or have lived in prison are the ones who know prison reality best; they are the true experts. I then selected undergraduate students from the State University of Maranhão (UEMA) to make up the team for the project, called *Another Vision*, obtaining extension scholarships for some of them. Among other duties, they had to read to those who could not read and write for those who could not write. However, at the end of the project, we noticed that they learned more than they taught (Biondi and Madeira, 2021; Viana, 2020; Garcia, 2021).

Unfortunately, the project was interrupted by the advent of the COVID-19 pandemic, which suspended all educational activities at APAC. We tried to maintain contact and develop remote activities with the prisoners, but we did not receive the necessary support from the prison administration. We were not even able to read to them the letter that the English prisoners who participated in Sacha and Andreas's project had written. However, the letter was later published as an appendix in a collection organized by Ross and Vianello (2021). In addition, Francisco produced a film about the project (Magalhães, 2020), called *Projeto Outra Visão: O Documentário* (Another View Project: The Documentary).

After the restrictions imposed by the pandemic were lifted, Sacha contacted me again, encouraging me to submit a proposal for a call for projects aimed at partnerships between universities and prisons. Since I had already started a research project at the São Luís Women's Prison Unit (UPFEM), I thought that would be the best place to propose the new edition of *Outra Visão*. I wrote the project, and fortunately, I was one of the successful candidates. If the first edition was done completely voluntarily, without any financial assistance to cover the project's expenses, this time I could count on funding from Bard Prison Initiative (BPI), in consortium with the Open Society University Network (OSUN) and the Incarceration Nations Network (INN).

I then began negotiations with the Penitentiary Administration Secretariat (SEAP). Unfortunately, some setbacks prevented us from taking the project to UPFEM. On the other hand, the doors of the Integrated Center for Penal Alternatives and Social Integration (CIAPIS) were opened to us, thanks to the invaluable partnership and support of the judge of the 2nd Criminal Enforcement Court, Dr Fernando Mendonça. The center is responsible for monitoring the execution of sentences for people deprived of their liberty in open regimes, house arrest, and parole.

In January 2023, with the support of the competent team at the CIAPIS Social Office, we opened registration for our course cycle. We received more than 40 applications and accepted all applicants. However, only 15 people attended the classes, which took place between February and April of the same year.

The courses

As mentioned earlier, after the first phase of the project (carried out at APAC at the time) was interrupted by the pandemic, we were able to conduct studies and develop our own methodology, taking into account the particularities of the prison environment in Maranhão. We then defined our work by offering extension courses, duly registered with UEMA, strictly following the institutional rules governing the offering of such courses, such as attendance and assessment control. These courses, which do not require prerequisites for registration, allow anyone interested to participate. Thus, even those who did not know how to read or write or had difficulty with it were able to participate in the activities and, later, in the production of this book, with the assistance of UEMA scholarship students. This is important, as mentioned, because it prevents further exclusion in the lives of those who have already been severely excluded.

We offered three short courses to incarcerated individuals: Social Education, Introduction to Social Sciences, and Introduction to Criminology. The courses lasted 20 hours and were held from Monday to Friday at CIAPIS. Topics covered included social inequality, the environment, gender and race, society and culture, law, crime, violence, and prison. Throughout the classes, we encouraged students to relate their life experiences to the academic content being taught. In this way, we aimed for them to see themselves as part of broader social processes and systems and to introduce new elements to analyses they were already developing, albeit informally.

At the end of each course, certificates were issued, duly registered with UEMA and signed by the university's Office of Extension. After this cycle, we moved on to the next stage of the project: the Ethnographic Writing Workshop, also lasting 20 hours. Since the writing process requires time to mature and develop, the classes were spaced out over longer intervals. Ethnographic writing, in short, consists of first-person accounts that describe a given social phenomenon in detail and analyze it, though it is not strictly biographical. In this workshop, we encouraged students to analyze their daily lives in prison, as well as life outside of it.

These were moments of intense exchange, where sharing experiences and expressing them led to critical reflection, both individually and collectively, on broader issues. Unlike merely living an experience, writing about it with critical reflection leads to greater self-awareness.

Among the students were men and women at different stages of the criminal process, serving sentences at various times and places. Comparing their experiences led to impressive analyses. Unfortunately, not all the richness of the intellectual exchanges we experienced during the courses was captured in writing. Reflections on the differences between men's and women's prisons, the changes in Maranhão's prison system over the last 15 years, the period before and after gang influence, slang, working conditions in prison, the constraints and violence of searches (especially body scanners), and the difficulties of finding employment post-incarceration were discussed. Each of these reflections, made during the classes, would greatly benefit the field of Criminology. This experience reinforced the importance of

Convict Criminology and investing in the intellectual training of those already experts in prison life.

Developments

At the start of this project, we aimed to stimulate interest in education and schooling among incarcerated individuals; to engage UEMA students in studying and working in the field of criminology; to foster critical thinking and intellectual autonomy; to promote reflection on the place of prisons and prisoners in society; and to offer new perspectives on the world we live in. Above all, we wanted to help incarcerated individuals feel like they are part of society and to show that education is a viable path for their lives. I believe we achieved all these goals. During the course, some students even enrolled in Youth and Adult Education.

However, two unforeseen developments occurred. The first came after contact with other projects supported by the same notice and with the Bard Prison Initiative, linked to Bard College, which offers undergraduate courses in American prisons. Inspired by our partners, Monica Piccolo (current Vice-Rector of Undergraduate Studies at UEMA) and I led the approval of a resolution at our university to create vacancies aimed at offering undergraduate courses to incarcerated individuals. We hope to begin in-person classes in Maranhão prisons soon.

This achievement was widely celebrated by the international community, which gathered in Buenos Aires for the First International Meeting on Higher Education in the Context of Deprivation of Liberty in April 2023. This meeting, where the partial results of Outra Visão were presented, brought together representatives from more than 25 universities from Latin America, Europe, the United States, and Africa. In addition to presenting their projects, learning from each other, and planning future partnerships, we learned firsthand about Argentina's pioneering experience in prison education (Bixio et al., 2016; Gutierrez, 2012; Parchuc, 2015).

A week before our departure for Buenos Aires, the Outra Visão Project received a visit from our English partners. Professors Sacha, Andreas, and Wendy came to São Luís, accompanied by seven master's students from the University of Westminster. During their stay in Maranhão, they met some of the authors of this collection, making for a truly intense experience. In June 2023, Francisco and I traveled to London for the Convict Criminology Symposium: Insider Prison Perspectives in Europe & the Americas, where we again spoke to an international audience about our project in São Luís.

Participation in these international events, made possible through our connection with the BPI/OSUN/INN call for proposals, led to the second unforeseen development: the formal insertion of Francisco into the academic debate. Arrested in 2003, Francisco remained provisionally imprisoned until 2008, when he was acquitted. During that period, he became a facilitator and consultant for my academic research. Although his invaluable contributions were detailed in my work (Biondi, 2016), his role was always informal and thus did not earn him the recognition he deserved. Now, under the framework of Convict Criminology, Francisco's decade-long leadership is being formally acknowledged, officially granting him the roles of researcher, educator, and author (see his article in this collection).

The chapters

During the course, some students got jobs, while others faced personal problems that prevented them from continuing. Seven stayed with us until the end. Of these, however, only five submitted their texts for this collection. Even so, more time for training and maturation would have been necessary for the texts to achieve the objectives initially set: to insert personal experiences in prison and crime into the broader academic debate. Although, as I mentioned above, this exercise was successfully carried out throughout the classes, the time allocated for writing the texts was insufficient to accomplish this task.

In order for the texts written in the project to formally enter the general debate (including the academic one) on prison, crime, and punishment, we considered it important to have the contribution of co-authors who could contextualize the discussion brought up by the reports. However, this does not diminish in any way the innovation and scientific contribution that the students of the Outra Visão Project are bringing. On the contrary, it validates them to the extent that it gives them the formats required by the academic world. The co-authorships promoted in this book were, above all, processes of exchange, in which the authors from academia were able to learn a great deal from the Outra Visão students. What we need now is to continue investing in offering them the scientific and academic tools so that they can express themselves and have their voices legitimized in society.

It is important to highlight that, while some of the reports were written, others were recorded and later transcribed. Some corrections were made to adapt the texts to the standard norms of the Portuguese language, while avoiding the distortion of the particularities and sophistications of the vocabulary specific to prison life and crime.

This collection has eight chapters, in addition to the introduction by Dr Fernando Mendonça, to whom we owe the conditions for carrying out the project at CIAPIS, and the preface by Prof. Sacha Darke, a kind of godfather to our project. To reaffirm our commitment to promoting academic production by people who have lived through the prison experience, in line with the Convict Criminology, the presentation of the chapters that follows will emphasize their main authors, that is, the students of the Outra Visão Project.

The first chapter, "Health and solidarity in São Paulo prisons," is the only one that addresses a prison reality outside the context of Maranhão. In it, Francisco Lopes de Magalhães Filho writes about the issue of health in the prison units where he has served, showing the strategies that prisoners use to deal with the lack of health services in the prison system.

The second chapter, "Before and after prison: Salvation stories," offers an impressive account of Edvan Ribeiro Matos's time in prison, narrating how he managed to save himself from a rebellion that occurred in Pedrinhas in 2008, and how this is linked to another form of salvation—religious salvation.

In the third chapter, "Work and redemption," Cristiane Santos tells us how her experiences in prison were influenced by the work she carried out, providing an important reference for anyone interested in the issue of prison labor.

The fourth chapter, "From FEBEM to Pedrinhas: Knowledge in crime," written by Alex Saraiva, illustrates how some choices made in childhood can lead to paths that are difficult to reverse. It also offers important contributions to understanding the dynamics of prisons in Maranhão.

In chapter five, "Daily life in the São Luís women's prison unit," Lúcia Santos Alves details the routines, interpersonal relationships, and humiliating, constant, and systematic searches that are part of life in the women's prison in the capital of Maranhão.

The sixth chapter, "Gender, prison, and torture: Beyond an androcentric perspective," provides an impressive account of the torture experienced by Elane Cristina Xavier da Silva at the time of her arrest, highlighting how such practices did not disappear with the end of the military dictatorship in Brazil.

Chapter seven was written by one of the project monitors, Ester Ametista Marques Mendes. Entitled "Convict criminology at Maranhão State University," the text discusses the area of criminology based on the author's experience in the project as a law student.

The final chapter, "Crossing borders: Exploring prison education projects in Convict Criminology in Brazil and the United Kingdom," was written by three of the University of Westminster's master's students. In it, Ella Walsh, Katharina Ammerer, and Rochell Bonnick share their impressions of the visit they made to the Outra Visão Project and CIAPIS in April 2023.

A few more words

The recidivism rate among Brazilian prisoners, although contro-versial, is quite high, with the number of repeat offenders being higher among those with less education (IPEA, 2015). In fact, studies prove the transformative power of education, reading, and writing in the lives of prisoners (Behan, 2014; Hughes, 2009; Piché, 2008). Despite this, initiatives, especially in Brazil, that go beyond technical courses, religious investments, or self-help teachings are rare. The idea that prison can house intellectuals only survived during the military dictatorship (1964–1985), and even then, left-wing intellectual prisoners made a point of differ-entiating themselves from ordinary prisoners. The basis for this differentiation is that some are granted the right to education and intellectuality, while others are relegated to the fate of man-ual, secondary, non-intellectual work, and this only when and if they are resocialized.

The Outra Visão Project goes against this hegemonic view. Fortunately, as I mentioned earlier, we have met several partners and supporters along the way who have helped us get this far, to the publication of this collection, to whom I am immensely grateful. But I hope that this book is only a provisional point of arrival; I hope that it becomes a point of propulsion for new pro-jects, new partnerships, new collaborations, and, who knows, new publications.

Above all, I hope, in line with the international network of which we are a part, that the academic debate on prison will increasingly include bibliographical references produced by people directly involved in prison life, by people who can, in fact, offer another view on the subjects of criminology.

Learning objectives

1. Recognize some particularities of Brazilian prisons.
2. Question the effectiveness of imprisonment policies.
3. Understand the importance of engaging with the narratives of people who have experienced the prison system.

1
Health and solidarity in São Paulo prisons

Francisco Lopes de Magalhães Filho[4]

Walkyria Biondi Lopes de Magalhães[5]

To Abba, in memoriam

Introduction

The Brazilian penitentiary system comprises 1,533 establishments with 461,026 places. However, the number of people deprived of liberty is 832,295. Of these units, 839 reported that they do not have doctors, 504 have only one doctor, and 190 have two or more (SENAPPEN, 2024).

Health is a constitutional right that must be promoted by the State in a universal and egalitarian manner (Ferreira, Silva and Godinho, 2020). Additionally, Interministerial Ordinance No. 1,777/2003, instituted by the Ministries of Health and Justice, approves the National Health Plan in the Prison System, and the Penal Execution Law provides for healthcare for prisoners and internees.

Regarding the Ordinance, Ferreira, Silva, and Godinho (2020, pp. 272) describe:

> These actions include the control of tuberculosis, hypertension, diabetes, leprosy, oral health, women's and children's health, mental health care, immunization program, diagnosis, counseling, and treatment of sexually transmitted diseases (STDs).

Furthermore, the 2003 Ordinance prioritized the renovation and equipping of prison units to provide medium-complexity care, in addition to organizing an information system on the health of the prison population and adopting harm reduction measures for drug users. It also provided for the allocation of R$40,008.00 per year for a team of health professionals to serve up to 500 people, while places with up to 100 people would have a budget of R$20,004 per year (Ministry of Health, 2003). This would be equivalent to an expense of R$80.01 to R$200.02 per prisoner, depending on the size of the prison unit.

The 1984 Penal Executions Law (Brasil, 1984) states that prisoners must receive preventive and curative care, with access to medical, dental, and pharmaceutical services. When these services are not possible, they must be provided elsewhere, as long as authorized by the management (Ferreira, Silva and Godinho, 2020). More recently, prenatal and postnatal care was included, extending to care for newborns (Law No. 11,942/2009), in addition to humane treatment during childbirth (Law No. 14,326/2022; Brasil, 2022).

However, despite legal provisions to promote health within prisons, in practice, the conditions are precarious. Many prisons are unsanitary, with closed, poorly ventilated, humid, hot, and overcrowded spaces conducive to the spread of various diseases (Ferreira, Silva and Godinho, 2020; Sánchez, Leal and Larouzé, 2016), as observed during the COVID-19 pandemic (Paixão, Maia and Cruz, 2021).

Research shows that people who enter the prison system often come from communities with precarious healthcare systems (Sánchez, Leal and Larouzé, 2016). When they enter the prison system, they become even more vulnerable to health problems due to the aforementioned conditions and the high prevalence of communicable diseases such as tuberculosis, hepatitis, and sexually transmitted diseases like syphilis and acquired immuno-deficiency syndrome (AIDS), caused by the HIV.

A survey of research addressing health in prisons conducted by Ferreira, Silva, and Godinho (2020) reports a 19.5% prevalence of the hepatitis B virus in the men's penitentiary of Ribeirão Preto, 14.47% of positive serology for the hepatitis C virus, 9.21% for HIV, and 2.63% co-infection in the women's penitentiary of Porto Alegre. In addition, the infection rate for tuberculosis increases with the length of imprisonment; the longer the prison term, the greater the chances of infection.

The authors present the following percentages regarding phys-ical health problems among the entire prison population in the state of Rio de Janeiro:

> [...] musculoskeletal, such as neck, back and spine pain (76.7%), joint dislocation (28.2%), bursitis (22.9%), sciat-ica (22.1%), arthritis (15.9%), fractures, cartilage, muscle and tendon problems (15.7%); those of the respiratory system, such as sinusitis (55.6%), allergic rhinitis (47%),

chronic bronchitis (15.6%), tuberculosis (4.7%) and others (11.9%)

In addition to these public health problems, the COVID-19 pandemic demonstrated how open, well-ventilated, and sanitized spaces make a difference in disease prevention (Barrouin et al., 2021). Various reports show how existing conditions, combined with sanitary measures, turned prisons into places of fear, violence, and pain for prisoners and their families.

The small, closed, and overcrowded cells became even more unhealthy with restrictions on sun exposure, a lack of water and hygiene products, and the use of containers that do not meet health requirements (Santos et al., 2020). In addition to physical deterioration, psychological health was severely affected by the suspension of visits (Barrouin et al., 2021).

Since prisoners were confined in areas highly prone to transmission, the number of reported cases and deaths from the novel coronavirus followed trends similar to those among free citizens but without the same access to care when needed (Barrouin et al., 2021). Data from DEPEN (2020) show that, since the beginning of the pandemic, 67,367 cases have been detected in the Brazilian prison system, with 293 deaths. However, only 366,166 tests were administered to the 832,295 incarcerated individuals. It is important to note that these data have been questioned by several researchers in the field (Prando and Godoi, 2020).

Based on the data presented, there is a clear gap between what the law mandates and what is implemented regarding healthcare in prisons. Next, we will present Francisco's experience during his imprisonment in the 2000s, demonstrating how, in the face of various deficiencies, prisoners themselves take on the responsibility of caring for each other's health.

Report

My first contact with nursing was through my mother, and later during my time in the army. I began serving in the armed forces in São Paulo and was later transferred to Manaus, where I managed to collaborate with doctors to provide care to some Indigenous people. When I was arrested, I started helping other sick and injured incarcerated persons, and that is what I intend to recount next.

When I arrived at the São Caetano public prison (São Paulo), I noticed many people needed medical care. So I started assisting the prisoners who required it. One day, a new prisoner arrived at the unit with bruises and a gunshot wound. He had already been to the hospital and the medical team had placed a tube in him to drain the fluids from the gunshot wound. Since the other prisoners knew I had some skill in outpatient care, this prisoner was placed in my cell so I could care for him more closely. His family brought him medicine stored in vials, which I administered while cleaning the wound with gauze and boric acid solution.

In addition to treating his wound, I also cleaned another incarcerated person's leg wound. I performed these treatments inside the shack (cell) every day until the day they were transferred. After that day, I never heard from them again.

In that same prison, on a particularly hot and sunny day, we saw a young man wearing a jacket. We found it strange and decided to ask why he was wearing warm clothes on such a hot day. We learned that, by accident, he had touched one of the "quiet" sheets (sheets that separate the cell to form small rooms for prisoners to have intimate visits). His cellmates interpreted this as disrespectful, and in response, they poured boiling water over his back, causing a severe burn.

Due to an escape plan that was underway, it was not possible to call for help. Therefore, he could not see a doctor, so I treated him by cleaning the area with boric acid and healing ointment. His entire back had third-degree burns, with secretions and infection, and he had a fever. Given the lack of resources, I began to think of alternatives. I remembered the campaigns in the 1980s that collected milk bags for people with burns because the material did not stick to the skin. The penitentiary provided milk in 100 ml bags for incarcerated persons at breakfast, so I started asking my fellow incarcerated persons for these. By joining the bags together, I could make a covering to protect the wound. Shortly afterward, I was transferred to another prison and lost contact with the boy.

I was transferred to DAKAR 7, a Provisional Detention Center (CDP). Although I could not intervene in many cases, people were dying due to a lack of care. One incarcerated person, responsible for distributing the lunch boxes, had tuberculosis but didn't know it. Over time, his symptoms worsened, and his health deteriorated. Eventually, the other incarcerated persons began to demand that the administration take action, shouting "PS!" (Pronto Socorro, the Brazilian expression to emergency medical help) to request that he be taken to the hospital. One day, he was carried away on a stretcher, unable to stand. The infirmary where he was taken was an isolated cell with a completely closed door, except for an opening for the eyes. It had an iron table typically used to transport corpses and no other resources. Due to these poor conditions, the young man died.

After being transferred again, this time to the São Bernardo CDP, I was assigned to the cleaning department (a cell where incarcerated persons are responsible for the internal administration of the pavilion). The cleaning department distributed food, deliveries, and incoming incarcerated persons, and guided each incarcerated person's movements. There, we began to identify incarcerated persons with diseases like AIDS, or those who had injuries or illnesses, so we could take necessary actions to help them and maintain the overall health of the population. Measures included searching for medication, requesting care to manage the HIV, and adopting sanitary rules.

Knowing the neglect of health within the prison system, we—the prisoners—looked for ways to support each other, as we were all in the same situation, united against the system, not each other.

One time, a young man arrived who had been shot in the mouth during an attempted bank robbery. His left cheek was swollen and red, with a large abscess from the infection caused by the bullet. Although he had been to the hospital, his wound had not been treated. We knew that if we requested an "ER" (medical care), he would be transferred to a small, unsanitary room they called an infirmary and would not receive proper care. Since the incarcerated persons knew I had already helped others, they asked me to treat his wound. I explained that to drain the abscess would be extremely painful, especially under the conditions we had. The young man assured me that he could handle the pain.

Normally, antiseptics and sterilized materials like scalpels, compresses, and gauze are used to drain an infection, but we had none of these, not even a knife to make the incision. I recalled my childhood, when my pencil sharpener would break, and I would use its blade. This childhood object now had a new purpose: a scalpel. I obtained a pencil sharpener from some friends and removed its blade. Then, I disassembled a ballpoint pen and heated the tip with a lighter until it nearly melted. I quickly fixed the pencil sharpener blade onto the end of the pen while the plastic was still soft. When it cooled, I had made my own scalpel.

I left the improvised scalpel and toilet paper aside and went to clean the area before the incision, but since we didn't have iodine, antiseptics, or even alcohol, we used deodorant. I made a small incision on the left side of the jaw, initially removing blood and later pus. The area gave off a foul odor. However, the secretion stopped coming out; I saw that the incision was obstructed by some white fragment that, at the time, I couldn't identify. With my fingers, I pulled out what we later found to be splinters of teeth and jaw, the probable sources of the infection. Since I couldn't leave these fragments, as they could lead to a new infection, I enlarged the incision, allowing more fragments to come out, and removed the rest with eyebrow tweezers. During this time, all the incarcerated persons in the pavilion were watching the procedure, as there was no private place to perform it.

After removing all the pus and debris from the site of the infection, I applied perfume (which contains alcohol) to the area to help with cleaning. I used fake stitches with adhesive tape and wrapped his face with a piece of the sheet that had been cut off, trying to prevent a new infection as much as possible, despite the precarious conditions. These were temporary measures, at least until I could get him to the emergency room, though we knew that getting him there would be very difficult.

This was one of the cases that shocked me the most because of the extent of the negligence regarding prisoners. In the state of São Paulo, there is a Criminological Observation Center, which operates as a prison hospital. However, I don't understand how people get there, as a young man with tuberculosis died without receiving any treatment. Then, they sent a young man who had been shot in the mouth to prison, without taking an X-ray or providing any treatment. They simply sent him to prison (and not to the prison hospital).

There are no health professionals in prison, even though prisoners have a constitutional right to access health care. The only people who take care of prisoners' health are the prisoners themselves, just as outside of prison, the population often helps each other when authorities do nothing.

In São Bernardo do Campo, an escape attempt was made but failed because guards began shooting at the prisoners trying to escape. Incredibly, one of them was shot in both feet. When I saw him, he was lying on the floor with his feet wrapped in sheets and said he was in a lot of pain. I told him that we needed to close the bullet holes, but the prison was in revolt. So I went to get cocaine to help with pain relief. Since I was well-known in the prison due to the time I had been there and also because I was in charge of distributing food, I went to another pavilion and asked an incarcerated person for ten grams of cocaine.

Returning to the pavilion, I gave the cocaine to the injured prisoner and applied some to the wounds. I saw that it would not be possible to close the wound and that attempting to do so could cause more damage, especially since there wasn't enough skin to suture. I checked to see if the blood was clotting and disinfected the area with perfume. Then, I cut some strips of bedsheets, bandaged his feet, and laid him down with his feet elevated. He would stay there until we could get help. One of the demands to end the rebellion was medical care, and since there were hostage employees to negotiate with, it was possible to arrange for the injured prisoner to be sent to the hospital.

After the rebellion, I was transferred again to the Pinheiros CDP and, after a few months, to the Vila Independente CDP. There, I met Abba and his partner. Abba was physically disabled and had no legs. They were accused of having murdered a Military Police sergeant during the attacks in São Paulo in 2006.

However, something caught my attention. The investigation report said that Abba's partner got off the motorcycle with a machine gun and shot the sergeant, who had no chance to defend himself, while Abba (who had no legs, remember) was driving the motorcycle.

I wondered how a judge could justify someone without legs being able to ride a 350 cc motorcycle, as was claimed in the investigation, especially since the motorcycle had a foot-operated gearshift. Furthermore, how would he be able to balance the motorcycle while standing up while his partner performed the action? Once again, the State ignored key facts and simply put him in jail, without providing any support for his special needs.

Accused of a crime he was physically incapable of committing, he was stuck in the prison system. Since help from the authorities was not forthcoming, we ourselves tried to assist him in every way we could. His partner and I helped with daily care routines, such as bathing and using the bathroom.

We noticed that he had pressure sores on his lower back due to the prolonged time he had to lie down, but we had nothing to clean the area with other than baths. The wound grew larger over time and began to emit a foul smell, which unfortunately nauseated others in the cell to the point where they could not eat. We managed to get some cachaça that the brothers in another cell had made. We started using it to clean the wound, but it was so deep that we could see his bone.

We shouted "PS," but no one came to help. Abba's condition worsened, and he began to have a fever, tremors, and fainting. We shouted "PS" repeatedly until a staff member came to yell at us through the gate (at the entrance to the ward). I complained that the staff didn't want to take care of him, wouldn't take him to the hospital, or give him any medication. I also said that they didn't even have the ability to provide any medication and that I was the one taking care of Abba. Unfortunately, the staff member ignored me.

After much insistence, we managed to get Abba out of there with the promise that they would take him to the Criminological Observation Center. However, they took him to an isolated, tiny, and completely locked cell, similar to the one I described earlier. He waited for them to take him to the hospital, but he remained there for days without receiving medical care or the company of those who had looked after him. Going through all his difficulties alone, he asked to return to the pavilion, but the staff in charge refused. He then sought help from another prisoner who, after spending some time in the infirmary cell next to his, was set to return to the pavilion. After that, the prisoners in the pavilion negotiated with the prison administration until they managed to get Abba back to his cell, where he received better care. When he returned and shared what had happened, it caused great outrage among the others, who protested to the administration.

During negotiations with the prison director, Abba was promised a transfer to the Criminological Observation Center, with assurances that they would take him by the end of the week. Around Wednesday or Thursday, they picked him up and took him there. Unfortunately, after about two or three months, we learned that he had died from a generalized infection.

What makes me most angry is what I usually call "shamelessness, bad character, scoundrelism, and rascality" when they claim that a fortune is spent on medical treatment for prisoners every year. According to SENAPPEN (2024), health care costs account for only 2.24% of the money spent on the prison system, which represents R$49.13 per prisoner per month. In comparison, SUS spends about R$3.83 per inhabitant per day, or about R$114.90 per month (CFM, 2020). Therefore, individual health care costs inside prisons represent less than 43% of what would be spent if the person were free.

In addition to these cases of bodily injury, I also assisted other incarcerated persons with dental care. After all, if we didn't have access to doctors, a dentist would be a luxury. One of the incarcerated persons I helped told me he had a terrible toothache and didn't know what to do. I suggested placing dipyrone on the tooth that was hurting, which in this case had a hole, and biting down on it with cotton. But this was just a palliative measure, not a solution, so he continued to suffer from the pain.

One day, I managed to get some Durepoxi, a compound that hardens when it dries, and it was the most viable option we had. I asked the incarcerated person with the toothache to lie down on the rock (bed) with his head on my lap. I wrapped toilet paper around his mouth and cleaned the dirt in and around the tooth with a sewing needle. Once the tooth was clean and dry, I applied the Durepoxi and pressed it with toilet paper, preventing it from getting wet and ensuring it adhered well. After that, he was pain-free for about two months, but eventually, the compound fell off, as it wasn't designed for that purpose, so we repeated the process.

I know it wasn't the right treatment, but we had no help there, so when we saw someone suffering in pain and needing assistance, of course, we helped. We wouldn't just stand by. What kind of human being would do that?

Furthermore, when you are in a closed space where all utensils are shared, someone who is sick or has an infection can spread it to others. Therefore, caring for others is not only an act of solidarity but also essential for the health of the group. Hygiene measures and individual health control are necessary for everyone's well-being.

Based on the report and data presented, the prison system does not provide basic health care to prisoners, who are forced to improvise, using the few resources they have to help one another.

2
Before and after prison: Salvation stories

Edvan Ribeiro Matos[6]

Karina Biondi[7]

Introduction

The presence of evangelical religions in the world of crime and prisons, or the presence of the world of crime in religions, in Brazil has been studied by several researchers (Birman, 2012; Dias, 2008; Lins and Silva, 1989; Machado, 2014; Marques, 2015; Medrado, 2016; Vital, 2015).

From the beginning of my research, the religious statements I encountered while studying in prisons caught my attention. In these facilities, neo-Pentecostal evangelical churches are the most prominent. For the prisoners I spoke with, the Catholic Church, especially through the Prison Ministry, is seen as one of the main bodies defending the rights of people in prison. One prisoner remarked:

> But they are very distant, a little arrogant, you know?
> They don't touch us, they don't ask how we are feeling…
> They are very formal. On the other hand, the brothers
> from the evangelical churches pay us more attention,
> they bring us spiritual comfort. Besides, they are here
> every week. And the Catholics only show up once in
> a while.

In summary, although they maintained relationships with both religions, the prisoners I spoke to indicated that while the Catholic Church was perceived as an institutional body for defending rights, evangelical religions served as sources of spiritual support. They conveyed an emotional connection that Catholics did not. Most importantly, they were more present in various dimensions.

Evangelical radio stations dedicate hours of programming to prisoners, and weekly services are held by evangelical preachers inside prison units. Biblical quotes, Christian references, and arguments based on religious teachings were prevalent in the statements made by prisoners throughout my research. There were also frequent readings of biblical passages that referenced the prison experiences of Jesus and some of his apostles. In this context, prison is seen as a test to which the prisoner is subjected, one that must be faced with courage, especially when God is conceived as the only judge—the only truly just being, capable of delivering "true justice." Among the most frequent statements, generally expressed as forms of consolation and motivation, are: "When man closes one door, God opens two," "Remember that God never gives us a cross heavier than we can carry, and that suffering feeds our courage more," and "Even though I am a sinner, the Lord loves me as I am."

This perspective allows us to treat crime as a sin like any other, equating them and nullifying any assessment of their gravity. As a pastor who conducted religious work in one of the prisons I studied stated, "There is no such thing as a little sin or a big sin; sin is sin." In this way, any sin constitutes a transgression of Christian principles and, as such, is capable of being forgiven by God, who is understanding and merciful. This understanding positions Him as the sole source of true justice—divine justice.

In Biondi (2022), I wrote the following lines:

> According to the religious discourse of evangelical preachers who visit prisons (many of them ex-prisoners who testify how they escaped the "life of crime"), prisoners who are able to surrender their lives to Christ acquire a freedom that is distinct from the right to come and go, which is the object of legal proceedings, and can be achieved even behind bars, in a spiritual dimension, by driving away the forces of Evil and curing the desire for worldly things that imprison people in a certain system of consumption.

Next, Edvan's report will describe in detail what these two prisons consist of, as well as their respective paths to salvation.

Edvan's report

On August 20, 2008, I was arrested. Before I get to that point, I'll tell you what happened beforehand.

I come from a humble family that suffered a lot, but what matters is that we succeeded in life. I am from Codó and came to São Luís when I was nine years old. Before coming here, I lived with an aunt because my mother gave three of her children to relatives at that time. She worked in the fields, and we earned our living from that. It was a time when things were very difficult financially, especially because the fruit of the palm tree was a year-round harvest. If we didn't stock up, we could go hungry. There were times when we ate white rice with *piaba* fish that we caught in a basket thrown into the river. When that wasn't possible, we lived off hunting and the *gong* that came inside the *babaçu* coconut.

This was a period of great suffering in my life. At the age of six, I was already working in the fields, raised in a rhythm of manual labor. When I was nine, I came to São Luís because my mother told me to gather all the children she had given birth to because her husband insisted on bringing all the scattered children together. And so it was done. I was a normal boy, quite polite, but as I grew up, I met the wrong friends, which led me to drugs. I used marijuana for the first time when I was 11 years old, and then I started going to rap parties, drinking, and prostituting myself. I also joined a São João gang, playing a TV character called Baby, which earned me my nickname, and it stuck.

As I grew up and got involved in the gang, I became known for having beaten up a person who was highly respected in the gang. This guy, leaving a party, found me and was coming to rob me and my girlfriend, but he came with a toy gun, and I was riding a bicycle. When he told us to pull over, he let the gun hit the frame of the bicycle. I was thinking and analyzing how I was going to disarm him, and then, in a moment of courage, I waited until he was even with me and immobilized him because I knew some capoeira moves. At that moment, two kids looked at us, and then I let him go because I had broken his nose and felt sorry for him. That's where my fame comes from: two gangsters passed by, saw the scene, and started spreading the word.

Many people started wanting to hang out with me, giving me drinks and drugs, and then I started getting involved in the drug trade. A guy and I started working hard. We would remove sand and rocks, and then we always did the job with our heads held high. We started saving money and buying larger quantities of drugs. We began to get involved in the world of crime through drug trafficking. We started buying marijuana in 25 g quantities; we would purchase it in Alto do Calhau, São Cristóvão, Forquilha, and Barreto. Then we opened a den in the woods of the Sampaio headquarters. Next to the Afonso Costa health center was our neighborhood, Baby's neighborhood, and ADM's neighborhood, my drug trafficking partner, who today, by the glory of God, is also an evangelical. But I tell all readers that if we hadn't embraced faith, we wouldn't be in this world anymore to tell this story.

We started selling and becoming quite well-known, and we were afraid of the police. Then we met a contact who supplied the den and lived near us, and he would leave the drugs for us in the hood. We started buying by the kilo and selling a lot; people came from far away to buy. This contact began making a killing, but I never grew in that business. My partner was growing, but since I liked reggae, I spent all my money on parties and women and didn't see any profit. When I started to get talked about a lot, my name became quite popular, and I was very afraid of being arrested. So the enemy gave me a strategy to change my nickname. I told people to start calling me Baby in the hood and Destaque on the streets.

That's when my time in prison began. On August 20, 2008, I was arrested. At that time, I had no tobacco or money. I only had enough money to buy new merchandise, and with the little profit I would make, I wanted to multiply it to buy the cell phone that my niece wanted to sell. So I asked him to sell me 25 g, but he locked himself in front of me and said he wouldn't sell it. I flattered him, and that was when he sold it to me. At that time, I had just bought a .32 caliber revolver, and I thought twice about taking it to the place where we used to smoke and sell. It looked like a field there, with overgrown weeds, so I decided not to take the revolver and went to meet the guys.

When I arrived, they asked me to take a hit, and I did: we started using drugs. Since we were talking very loudly, two police officers who were passing by in a patrol car heard the noise we were making and followed the trail that led to our den in the middle of the woods. Then one of the police officers came up behind me and arrested me, shouting for no one to run because the police had arrived. I thought it wasn't serious; every now and then, a guy would show up with a suggestion, that is, someone would show up wanting to intimidate us so we wouldn't smoke there. But when I turned around, with the marijuana cigarette in my mouth, I saw that it was the real police, pointing a .38 at my head. They forced us to the ground and put their leg on my head.

They started looking for more drugs besides the ones in my hand. They asked where the gun was and whose drugs were there. Since no one answered, one of the officers fired a shot, which went straight to my head; the dirt rose up and hit me in the eye. Then I thought, if I don't tell him that these drugs are mine, he'll kill me right here and say I resisted arrest, so I told him that the drugs were mine. They started searching again, turned everything over, and then found more drugs. These drugs belonged to the "plane" (an employee at the drug dealing point) of my partner, who was making his way in the business. The police found the drugs and started asking who they belonged to. They asked me, but I said I didn't know who they belonged to; I only knew that the drugs he had grabbed from my hand were mine. Since no one said anything, they grabbed one of the people closest to the drugs; it was a user who was there to buy and ended up staying to smoke.

The two of us were then taken together from the woods to the police car. The police officers who were there and knew us said we were good people, but the ones who caught us said there was no deal. So we went down to the police station and were detained there. We stayed there overnight, and the next day, two prison guards arrived and said, "From today on, you are prisoners of justice." That was when my life in prison began.

From there, I was taken to the Pedrinhas Triage Center to spend 15 days in triage before being assigned to a prison cell. During this period, there was an evangelical brother, also a former drug dealer, and when we arrived, he started talking about Jesus to the two of us, but neither I nor the other guy paid attention. In addition to discussing Jesus, he talked about the prison's pace, the slang, and the rules, but I didn't pay much attention to anything he said. Since it was our first time being arrested, we were, as they say today, green bellies; we didn't know anything about prison. We were sent to the pavilion, while this brother stayed in triage because he was going to be transferred, as the prison was full.

The boy who was arrested with me started to throw accusations against me to gain favor with the other prisoners, claiming that I had thrown drugs at him, which I had not done. In fact, I had admitted to my own drug use, while he was near the boy's drugs. He accused me because we were involved in the same case; it was just one case since we were arrested together. However, when we reached the cellblock, he went to one section and I went to another. The prisoners in his cell and those in mine wanted to know why we were there. He claimed it was because I had set him up, that I had informed on him. Because of this, when I was telling the truth to the prisoners in my cell, they began to doubt me. I confronted him a couple of times, as he was speaking to me, but another incarcerated person would interrupt, which prompted the first one to claim that I was denying him a chance to respond, giving him a reason to confront me. He said that the "car of the biriba" ran me over, so I got run over a couple of times in prison; I got caught.

On one occasion, a guy in prison kicked me with a flying kick, nearly causing me to hit the back of my head on the stone bed in the prison. But I believe that all of this was the enemy knowing that I was going to give my life to Christ, that I was going to surrender to the Lord Jesus Christ, so he was already starting to work to take me down before I could accept Jesus. My sister was evangelical and prayed a lot for me when she was pregnant, and she always sent me those little discipleship magazines from the Assembly of God, which I read frequently.

Since the prisoners wanted to know who was telling the truth, they said, "Tomorrow, in court, we'll find out who's telling the truth and who's not." They were eager to see bloodshed. The next day, while sunbathing in the courtyard, they put us face to face. The guy who was arrested with me started pointing at me, saying that I had thrown drugs at him, and I told him to be a man for once in his life and tell the truth. I stated that I was there because they caught me red-handed, while he was there because he fell near the other guy's drugs. He continued to insist that I was lying, pointing his finger in my face. At that moment, since I wasn't an evangelical yet, I closed my fist and punched him. The other incarcerated person in his cell tried to punch me, but I ducked, and then he came at me. The one with the knife was there, but by the grace of God, I was saved, and an officer looked at us and fired a shot between us.

Everyone dispersed, and the officer came to us asking who started the trouble. I had a flashback of what I had been told: that I shouldn't obey the officers or do what they told me, but I also remembered what I had been through in that prison. As soon as I got there, I went to sharpen a knife for them. Remembering that, I wondered if this knife could really be intended for me. The officer told me to leave, and the prisoners started telling me not to go, but I left the courtyard. The officer instructed the other officer to leave too, but he didn't.

I then requested to be moved to another cellblock, where there were another drug dealers from my neighborhood. At that time, prisoners sought to join people they already knew (usually those who lived in the same neighborhood as them before being arrested), with whom they formed bonds of solidarity, help and mutual protection. With the emergence of prison collectives (such as Comando Vermelho, Primeiro Comando da Capital,

Bonde dos 40), this dynamic changed, but at that time it was like that. .. However, the officers didn't want to transfer me, saying they wanted to hold me hostage in that cellblock. This was because my cousin had gone to bring me clothes on a weekday, but he didn't come in since it wasn't visiting day. He had an acquaintance who was a prison officer, and he gave the clothes to this officer to deliver to me. With that, I imagine they thought I knew the officer. So, they decided to place me in a cellblock known as "safe" (where incarcerated persons' lives are at risk if they are in contact with other prisoners).

When I entered this pavilion, I met the young man who had initially spoken to me about Jesus. He explained that he had not been transferred and was already prophesying and calling me brother, although I was not. We agreed to talk more the next day in the courtyard, as there would be sunbathing in that pavilion. That was when my second prison sentence began.

I met the boy again while we were sunbathing, and he started talking to me about Jesus. We walked around the courtyard while he spoke. Meanwhile, the other incarcerated persons engaged in their activities: playing ball, getting their hair cut, playing dice. He began discussing God, even though he didn't have a Bible.

He said a lot to me, without knowing me, and I wanted to draw my own conclusions. Then, on Sunday, my mother came to visit me. Without having accepted Jesus yet, just to see her reaction, I said that I had accepted Jesus. At that, she frowned at me. I realized that it wasn't my mother who was there, but the entities that accompanied her. I then understood that the conversation with my brother made sense; after all, what mother wouldn't be happy when her son says he accepted Jesus? Everyone knows that Jesus is a good thing, and I was able to conclude that the man was right about what he was saying.

In John 8:32, it says that "You will know the truth, and the truth will set you free." And then, my dear brothers, I believe that after she left, Jesus had an encounter with me. When I knelt down to accept the name of Jesus Christ, I expressed my desire to accept Jesus, and all the weight and pain in my heart began to leave me, causing me to cry. I truly began to empty myself of the old creature, of the old man. God started to remove all those thoughts of killing and revenge from my heart, and then I was guided by that brother.

But before that, I began to live a life of persecution inside the prison because the enemy, who knew that my soul was weak, started using the prisoners themselves to provoke me, to take away my blessing, and to make me return. I went through these tribulations. Every now and then, I was beaten, but the worst part was during a rebellion.

They started saying that "the jail was about to break," but I didn't know what breaking the jail meant. Then they made me shake the bars, and we did so every night, shaking the jail by rattling the bars.

One of those nights, while we were shaking the bars, the jail broke. According to the rules of the jail, when it breaks, all the prisoners run to the safe pavilion to take hostages from those who are inside to behead them or kill them, as many of them have debts to drug dealers and are discriminated against. But many are there because they don't want to get into trouble; they just want to pull through, but they end up there. As the saying goes, everyone pays for something. Then they broke the chain and started coming toward the safe pavilion. At that point, we also tried to break out to evacuate to the courtyard for an escape, but we were unable to break the wall. In our desperation, we began to panic because we knew that the three pavilions were coming for us, intending to make us their victims.

As we grew more desperate, we had an idea when there was only one padlock left to break to access our cell. It was already midnight and nearing dawn. The idea was to start banging pots and pans against the bars, and each cell began making noise with pots and pans. The GEOP (Special Penitentiary Operations Group), which was stationed in front of the prison, heard the shouting and drumming and came in, but they arrived shooting at everyone. By the time we explained that we weren't the ones breaking into the jail, three prisoners from our cell had already been shot—one in the eye, another in the throat, and another in the leg. They then attempted to control the other enraged cells, putting us in a tight spot and not allowing them to get through the gate. Now, imagine us spending the rest of the night in the cell while they shouted constantly, even forcing open the large gate that was there.

This all happened at the Pedrinhas CCPJ in 2008. At that time, each pavilion held around 150 to 250 prisoners. I know that the three pavilions together housed more than 500 prisoners. Then what happened? They broke down the gate and came after us, trying to grab us in the courtyard. Some of us began climbing over a screen and jumping from up there into the courtyard. The courtyard was surrounded by a warehouse that served as a place of prayer and some other rooms. What separated the courtyard from the warehouse was a large screen, a fence. So we started throwing ourselves, jumping, and climbing over the fence. They began pulling us by the legs, throwing us to the ground, and stabbing us in all that chaos. Thank God I managed to climb over the screen and throw myself from there. Thankfully, I didn't get a scratch, but many prisoners were injured during that time.

So we stayed in the warehouse. Now, just imagine, there were ten cells in just one pavilion, with more than 150 men crammed into one warehouse. We endured that horrible heat and agony, and my brother was also instructing me the whole time.

In that place, God gave me a dream or a revelation; I don't know what it was. I was squatting down, my head between my legs, and I took a 15-minute nap. While I was sleeping, God showed me a rebellion, and in it, I was running away with another boy who was far away until I stopped in front of a black hole—an abyss—and I stood there, immobilized, looking at it. The boy behind me wanted to jump, and I told him, "Don't jump!" That scared me, and I woke up, keeping that in my mind.

In that dream, God made me understand that if I continued living the life I was leading—in the world of drug trafficking, in the world of crime—I would not have many more days to live. God had already given me several opportunities and deliverances when I was on the street, partying in the early hours of the morning, and He made me realize that if I had not accepted Jesus at that moment, I could have died in that rebellion. I felt that was my last opportunity.

As they were fixing the pavilion so we could return, we stayed in that warehouse for about a week until we were taken back. One day, on a Friday, my release order arrived. Since I was a first-time offender, I was supposed to spend six months there, but God was so wonderful! He heard my prayers. I fasted, humbled myself before God, and made a sincere covenant with Him: if He took me out of there, I would testify to His name and share His love with everyone I met. Thus, I sealed my covenant with God, and He was so faithful! I asked Him to release me on October 20, and on October 9, the Lord took me out of that place.

I didn't even spend three full months in prison; I arrived in August and left at the beginning of October. However, the time I spent there felt like decades, centuries; it was a very bad experience. Yet, I learned a lot in prison. At that time, I was starting to use crack, but in prison, there was more merla, which the other prisoners produced, and I observed the whole process. I also learned how to make an electric stove and do crafts.

In prison, I learned many things, including the importance of respect for coexistence, that everyone must respect each other's space, that people need to be humble, and that we should treat each other like family because everyone is in the same situation of suffering. Everything needs to be agreed upon, everything has to be discussed, and we must share.

Routine inside the prison

When you arrived at prison, you were assigned to a cell. Some cells had other incarcerated persons who wanted to make you clean until you got out. Others worked in shifts, where each day a different incarcerated person was responsible for cleaning. In some cells, there were specific duties; for example, some were responsible for getting coffee, others for lunch and dinner, and only one was responsible for cleaning the bathroom. To get coffee, you had to wake up early and take a shower; otherwise, that was already a reason for to get beaten by other prisoners. Whoever was responsible for cleaning the bathroom had to scrub the walls and everything else thoroughly, ensuring the toilet had no slime because it would be checked.

As a pastime, there were games: some played cards, others played dice, some read books, and I used my time to delve into the word of God. Thus, the days went by inside the prison. At 5:30 or 6:00 a.m., breakfast arrived; at 11:30 a.m., lunch arrived; at 3:00 p.m., a snack was provided; and at 6:00 p.m., dinner was served.

Every fifteen days, a person could receive visitors, but only when the cell was not under punishment. Punishments occurred when something illegal was found inside the cell or in someone's cell. When someone left for the infirmary or somewhere else, they would leave the cell and have to squat three times. Upon returning, they had to repeat the same procedure. At that time, we were allowed to sunbathe twice a week; I don't know if that has changed.

There were times when the GEOP or the agents themselves would come in and surprise us during unannounced searches. They would arrive with bombs and pepper spray and send everyone to the back of the cell. Anyone found in possession of anything illegal, such as a chemical substance, drugs, or a "parrot" (cell phone), would be punished for fifteen days in an isolated cell, lose the right to receive visitors, and be subject to a PDI (Internal Disciplinary Process).

That was my routine inside prison—an experience that allows me to speak about what prison is like. Thanks to the word of God, I changed significantly and transformed into who I am today, leaving a life of crime and even adapting my speech to avoid using slang.

Freedom

After I was released, my case continued to unfold, so another story emerged from there. On the day the lawyer released me, he said, "Look, you can live your normal life from home to church, from church to home," but he didn't tell me that I had to keep signing. I'll share another part that will help you understand this second part.

Time passed, and I had been in the presence of God for a year. I got married, and after six months, my wife became pregnant. My son was about to turn one when I was sentenced to a closed regime. I was desperate! What would become of my son? At that time, none of my older children lived with me. What was I going to do?

God used a woman who said that she would raise funds to solve this case, so we spoke to a lawyer, someone we knew, who was also the cheapest we could find. He asked for R$5,000 to appeal the sentence. According to the sentence, I was facing four years and six months in a closed regime, a process that I am still going to sign today. This lawyer wanted R$2,000 as a deposit to file the paperwork, but we didn't have the money.

At that moment, God began to use people who donated and raised funds until we managed to gather two thousand reais. We filed an appeal, but there was another young man involved in the same case who, in order to be acquitted, blamed me entirely. With a good lawyer, paid for thanks to his mother's work relationship with a councilman, he harmed me, made me go to jail, and was acquitted while I was convicted. My lawyer couldn't find any loopholes for my release; none of the prosecutors or the judge wanted an acquittal or a new trial. So, the lawyer appealed in Brasília and managed to reduce my sentence from four years and six months in a closed regime to four years and four months in a semi-open regime. As a result, I was granted the right to serve my sentence in an open regime on the streets. While in a closed regime the prisoner must remain in prison facility all the time, in an open regime he doesn't need to stay there. He can go home, work, study. However, he is still serving his sentence and, therefore, has some restrictions, such as not being able to leave the city, in addition to needing to report periodically to the judge of his case.

I won't say that I liked being arrested; I didn't! But if I hadn't been arrested, I wouldn't be the person I am today. God was so wonderful to me because even though everyone in my neighborhood knew I had been arrested, I received a job offer a week after being released. You know that for all those released from the prison system, the doors are usually closed, but God was so wonderful and opened the door to employment for me, sending someone to my house to ask if I wanted to work as a caretaker.

I received a lot of criticism because I had a reputation for taking other people's things, for being a thief, and when I was also known for drug trafficking, no one would open doors for me. I was feared in society, among the "crooks," but this man gave me a vote of confidence, and since I was already in the presence of God, I wanted to start making a difference.

I decided to work with this man, and I thank God for putting him in my life. He had the patience to teach me various professions because I was a laborer who took on the most manual tasks. I don't have a certificate in any of these professions; however, I can do them easily. The house I live in was built by my own hands. I learned construction; I'm a bricklayer. I can turn a house over with a key, work with electricity, and handle all the installation work inside the house, for the glory of God! I also learned how to weld with him, as well as how to install ceilings and frames.

Since I learned several trades, I can now work independently. I am a daily cleaner, self-employed, and I live well, thank God. I have five children: two from before I became an evangelical and three from after. They are a blessing in my life.

After I left there, I began to dedicate myself to the ways of the Lord, seeking to evangelize and strengthening myself in the presence of God.

In 2009, there was another rebellion in the same prison where I was, and at that time, factions were already beginning to form. Several people were beheaded there, including prisoners who were in safe custody. God once again made me understand that if I had not accepted Him, I could have been one of the dead people reported in the newspaper. This was the deciphering of the dream, the revelation in which God showed me a black hole.

If I hadn't accepted Jesus, no one would know a little about the story that I'm telling for this publication. I know that it will help many in the journey of some of my brothers—those who truly want to leave the life of crime and become resocialized individuals, good people of character.

Prison, in my view, takes someone away from their comfort zone, from the comfort zone of their family, and isolates them in order to punish them. It takes away their right to privacy and their right to interact with others; these are forms of punishment in addition to the punishment of paying for their actions. It excludes a person from society as a form of punishment, and all of this is classified by the responsible bodies. Consequently, it is also a prison of the soul, in which the person is imprisoned by their crimes and sinful acts, both before God and before men. For me, this is prison.

I can talk about what prison is because I was imprisoned—both in crime and in drugs, prostitution, and alcoholism, and all of this led me to prison. Today, I can tell you that I am free in both senses.

The "good" part of this experience was that I made new friends and learned things I didn't know. With God's help, I consider myself resocialized and ready to face the world outside.

3
Work and redemption

Cristiane Santos[8]

Ester Ametista Marques Mendes[9]

Cristiane's report

Here, I will share how I suffered in prison. On November 23, 2018, I arrived at the São Luís Women's Prison Unit (UPFEM). I remember that day as if it were today. I was very scared, looking at everyone and hearing many women screaming. I asked myself, "My God, what kind of place is this?" I had no idea I was in a women-only prison. I never imagined in my life that there were so many women deprived of their freedom, to the extent that there were prisons just for them.

When I first arrived, they took me to a room and asked me several questions. They inquired about what led me to commit the crime, where I lived, and details about my case. Then, they took me to a search room. That's when the prison officer instructed me to enter the room, undress completely, and squat three times facing forward and three times facing backward. I felt really uncomfortable about all of this; it was embarrassing. To make matters worse, the prison officer treated me brutally. This made me so nervous that I ended up doing the whole procedure wrong, and I had to repeat it several times until I got it right, that is, until I performed the movements and actions exactly as the officer instructed. I was even more frightened when I saw a large number of women coming and going in that room. I wondered if I would have to go through all of this every time I was taken out of my cell for some activity or service. And indeed, I had to endure this embarrassment every time.

After I completed the procedure, they took me to a cell. I had no idea at that moment that I would experience so many things there. Upon entering the cell, a woman who, I was later told, was very dangerous, looked at me and said, "Welcome to the Barbie hotel." I started to cry. Then she looked at me and said, "There's no point in crying. I think it's better if you don't stay like that because the other girls won't like it." In prison, when one girl cries, it makes the others feel sad too, as the reasons for one girl's tears are usually the same reasons the others cry. Days went by, and I was still learning to hold back my tears while feeling completely lost in time; the hours dragged on.

After 10 months, my sentence arrived. I left the provisional detainee ward and moved to the convicted women's ward. There, I faced several struggles, as I was persecuted by some incarcerated persons. However, despite the great difficulties, I persevered. I started working in the ward, distributing meals in the cafeteria. I worked in that sector for five months.

Every day, we woke up very early, took a shower, and from that point on, the noise and banging of plates began, which almost drove me crazy. This was because the incarcerated persons spent the whole day in their cells. They could only sunbathe once a week for two hours. To pass the time, the women banged on the plates, communicating with each other, shouting, and talking. In addition, every time the doors opened and closed, the sound of metal banging echoed throughout the gallery. The doors opened and closed non-stop, which is why the sounds of locks, bars, plates, and metals were relentless.

The nights were a bit calmer. First, we would say our prayers, form a circle, and begin reading the Bible and singing hymns. Each prisoner, with their own religion, would pray in their own cell, allowing everyone to hear each other and sing praises together. When we finished, it was time for the canteen (the container where the food was served). Most of the time, we didn't even eat the food because it was horrible. Often, the food arrived sour and spoiled; the meat was greenish, the chicken had feathers, and the food smelled bad. After the girls went to bed, sadness, tears, and despair would set in. Initially, I couldn't sleep or eat; I would just cry. I spent sleepless nights, thinking that it was all over for me. Fortunately, I always had the support of my family and the brothers and sisters from the church I attended at the time, which helped me a lot.

The incarcerated persons who received visits were all very anxious for the day to see their families. Visits took place from 8 a.m. to 12 p.m. on weekends. Despite the joy of seeing their families, the day of inspection was also a day of suffering. All the incarcerated persons were taken out of their cells and brought to the courtyard while the cells were searched one by one. After the procedures were completed, we returned to our cells and had to tidy everything up because everything was a mess. The prison staff would throw the mattresses on the floor to step on them, rummage through our personal items, and scatter everything on the floor. In short, it was complete chaos. Everything that was not allowed in the cells was confiscated. If there were ten of us in a cell, for example, there could only be ten towels; the sheets were the same, and even our underwear was counted. Any prohibited items were removed. The Internal Disciplinary Processes (PDIs) were enforced when something illegal was found, and then the prisoner was sent to solitary confinement for a few days.

The period when the COVID-19 virus arrived in Brazil was very sad. Due to the virus, visits were suspended, and we were unable to see our family members. Only the items our family members brought us were allowed into UPFEM. I suffered a lot because I had no news of my family, especially my daughter. During this time, I ended up in the UPA (Health Emergency Care Unit) because my back was in severe pain, and I could barely walk. When I returned from medical care at UPFEM, I was placed in isolation due to COVID. We had to stay in isolation for 14 days to avoid the risk of infecting other incarcerated persons. Since there was no place to isolate ourselves, we were taken to the area designated for incarcerated persons with bad behavior, which was not my case, and I suffered greatly because of that. There, we didn't see sunlight, couldn't go out for anything, and the conditions were dirty and dark. Furthermore, spending 14 days in isolation without hearing from my family and without the support of my cellmates made my suffering even worse.

Thank God, I didn't have to stay in isolation for the entire 14 days. After eight days, I returned to the pavilion. After a month, I started cleaning the pavilion corridor, even though I had intense back pain. It was very hard work. I felt disgusted because there were so many rats and feces. But I didn't see any alternative, as this was the way to escape that suffering as quickly as possible. I worked in cleaning for a month. I wasn't paid for this work, but I received a sentence reduction for the days I worked. One day, the management called me. That's when I received great news: a job opening in external service had come up, which guaranteed that my semi-open prison status would no longer be just a right but would become effective. I was overjoyed.

I went to work at the Casa da Mulher Brasileira in a general services role. I was treated well, and I felt comfortable and at ease with the employees there, even those who were not part of the system. I spent a year working during the day and sleeping in the prison. After a year of external service, my release warrant arrived. I went home to start a new life from scratch. Today, I am very happy, and I always pray for the other girls who are still at UPFEM. I pray that they leave there as warriors—new women, ready to face life outside.

Discussion

Cris's report highlights a significant emphasis on the perspective of work in the prison context. In this way, we will begin an analysis pertinent to the topic, with the objective of providing a reflection from the perspective of those who have already been involved in the reality of prisons and work while incarcerated. In order to understand the dynamics and challenges faced by ex-prisoners in the prison system, it is essential to prioritize the experiences reported by them. This approach allows for a more comprehensive and empathetic analysis, taking into account the experiences and obstacles encountered by those who have gone through this reality. In this way, we seek to offer a vision of the importance of work in the resocialization process while recognizing the complexity of prison conditions and the challenges faced by incarcerated persons after their release.

Several thinkers discuss work concerning society. According to Marxist theory, for example, a dual relationship of representation is understood in the context of a capitalist society. Marx understands the concept of man and work in a way that recognizes it as a substantial activity. According to Morin (2001, pp. 16), "the work process, as well as its fruit, helps the individual to discover and form his identity." Thus, we can understand that work and the process of producing goods and services influence our thoughts, in addition to the freedom and independence that we possess. The understanding of the subject has several aspects and interpretations; let us see:

> The concept that work and the meaning of human life are directly linked has been present in Western thought for a long time, not only for the purpose of organizing the workforce within industries that have recently been booming, but also as a way of disciplining a poor portion of society. (Vieira and Stadtlober, 2020, pp. 81).

From a correctional perspective, labor was incorporated into European incarceration systems as a measure to resocialize so-called "delinquents." For Foucault (1977), the criminal execution process became an autonomous sector, which had a complex social effect, and there was no longer any need for torture as a form of punishment, primarily due to the context of major changes related to the industrial revolutions. According to the author:

> It might be objected that imprisonment, confinement, forced labour, penal servitude, prohibition from entering certain areas, deportation — which have occupied so important a place in modern penal systems — are 'physical' penalties: unlike fines, for example, they directly affect the body. But the punishment-body relation is not the same as it was in the torture during public executions (Foucault, 1977, pp. 11).

In this way, various punishment regimes are imposed on individuals in a coercive and repressive manner, aiming to make them docile and useful. This type of social control over the body also acts in a corrective manner on the population in general.

The idea was then fostered that the only way to protect society from criminals would be through harsh sentencing practices, leading to more people being sent to prison. One of the immediate consequences of this is the need to build more prisons. When we connect prison and work, we notice that the majority of those incarcerated are black bodies transformed into a source of profit, indicating that the perpetuation of prisons may be, among other things, in the interests of companies.

In the case of the Pedrinhas Complex in São Luís do Maranhão, there is an intense focus on manual labor among incarcerated persons, both men and women, such as making clothes for the state through knitting factories inside prisons or working in concrete block factories. It is worth noting that in Brazil — as in many former slave states — the prison population changed drastically after the abolition of slavery, becoming predominantly black. According to Angela Davis (2003), the transition that occurred at that time paved the way for the easy acceptance of prison populations, which are predominantly black. The author makes it clear that black bodies are "dispensable in the 'free world,' but are seen as an important source of profit in the prison system" (Davis, 2003).

This change in perception regarding prisons as a punishment system occurred mainly after the shift in understanding of the individual as a being holding formal rights and freedoms. Consequently, punishment through prison was understood as a form of resocialization that would produce reformed and improved individuals for society, yet it still produced delinquent individuals. The French and American Revolutions were primarily responsible for entrenching these new ideals. It is important to emphasize, however, that these ideals were not extended to women. This directly affected the imprisonment of female bodies, as the "public status of individuals holding rights was largely denied to women" (Davis, 2003).

While prison emerged as a humanized measure of penance, offering men a chance to regain their freedom through reflective methods, work, and religion, it was understood that the work performed by individuals is a bearer of dignity, morality, and ethics, rescuing feelings essential for the construction of a new life. In this context, however, "women were not able to go through this process of redemption" (Davis, 2003) as they were not considered individuals with rights, often remaining confined to the private sphere and directed to psychiatric hospitals, mental institutions, and religious spaces. After several changes aimed at humanizing punishment—changes that were late in relation to women—Brazilian incarceration continued to employ a correctional model focused on work activities, with the goal of harshening the sentence, until the twentieth century, which hindered the creation of the Penal Executions Law (LEP) in 1984 (Brasil, 1984).

The law initiated a process of jurisdictionalization of the penal system, allowing for its execution through punishment and monitoring by a judge. This systematic modification arose from the need to legitimize a path toward greater democracy in the area, theoretically aligning with international treaties aimed at preserving the rights of convicted individuals, such as the Standard Minimum Rules for the Treatment of Prisoners established at the First United Nations Congress on the Prevention of Crime and the Treatment of Offenders (United Nations, 2015).

According to Article 28 of the LEP, the work of incarcerated persons, regarded as a social duty and a condition of human dignity, has both educational and productive purposes. The difficulties that convicted individuals encounter in obtaining work express a restriction of rights, demonstrating legal inefficiency regarding its fulfillment (Ribeiro, 2014). According to the aforementioned law, the provision of work to incarcerated persons is a state obligation, as there is a condition of proposed benefit through the fulfillment of work activities, necessitating the allocation of the means for its implementation. Therefore, "Work is, therefore, a subjective right of the prisoner in relation to the Public Authorities, but penal establishments and prisons are generally devoid of sufficient material and human resources to offer decent work to all incarcerated persons" (Alvim, 1991, pp. 86).

As stated initially, although torture instruments were used in the past, problems of exclusion and social segregation persist today, hindering the reintegration of prisoners into society. Even though prison work currently aims to reintegrate prisoners, and despite government efforts to draft the law, we can observe, as noted above, that the available positions for external service are scarce. For example, only after one year within the system was an opportunity offered to the former incarcerated person, despite her good behavior, involvement in available internal activities, and demonstration of her aptitude for work in accordance with the criteria required in Article 37 of the LEP:

> The provision of external work, to be authorized by the establishment's management, will depend on aptitude, discipline and responsibility, in addition to the minimum completion of 1/6 (one sixth) of the sentence. (Brasil, 1988).

According to the Maranhão Prison Monitoring and Inspection Unit (UMF-MA), in the latest data survey released in 2020, out of 451 women deprived of liberty who study and work in prison units, only 60 were employed (UMF, 2020). In parallel with the low demand for external work and the criteria applied for a prisoner to qualify and be selected, issues such as remuneration for the prisoner (when this possibility exists in addition to the remission of sentence through working hours) also remain problematic. Additionally, the opportunities that are not available in the environment outside the prison contribute to this issue, as the predominant societal perception regarding the resocializing purpose of prison institutions is skeptical, creating significant obstacles for reintegrating ex-prisoners into the community.

This prejudiced attitude results in numerous challenges, such as the scarcity of job opportunities and a lack of acceptance in the spaces they frequent, leading to marked social discomfort. The adversities faced by prisoners within the penitentiary system transcend the work sphere, and when these individuals are released, they find no prospects for a life beyond what has already been offered to them. This socially stigmatized perception perpetuates a vicious cycle in which reintegration into society becomes increasingly challenging.

The meetings held by the "Outra Visão" project were attended by seven to twelve graduates interested in sharing their experiences and acquiring the knowledge offered during the courses. With the exception of one student employed in external work (as he was still in a semi-open regime), the others did not have formal employment, and even those who were working faced the issue of not being properly paid and being exploited in informal activities. Furthermore, it was found during several meetings that when they had the opportunity to enter formal employment under the Consolidation of Labor Laws (CLT), they were immediately overlooked upon revealing their status as graduates.

In this context, the meetings provided a space for former incarcerated persons to share their experiences and challenges in their search for a place in the job market. Most participants reported difficulties in finding formal employment, which led them to accept informal jobs with insufficient pay to meet their basic needs. This reality underscores the importance of public policies that promote inclusion and appreciation for former incarcerated persons, as well as raising awareness and sensitivity in society and companies regarding their reintegration. Overcoming the stigmas associated with being a former incarcerated person is essential to enable the construction of a more just and egalitarian society, offering real opportunities for reintegration into the job market and the community for those who have served their sentences and are seeking to rebuild their lives.

Regarding prisoner remuneration, § 1 of Article 29 of the LEP states that "The work of the prisoner will be remunerated according to a previous table and cannot be less than 3/4 (three-quarters) of the minimum wage" (Brasil, 1988). Such a provision further disfavors the resocialization process and facilitates the exploitation of prisoners under the guise of the resocializing premise of work, thus undermining its main purpose. Cabral and Silva (2010, pp. 165) argue:

> If the objective of prison work is the resocialization of the prisoner, receiving a salary below the minimum wage frustrates its purpose, insofar as the prisoner receives less than any other worker solely and exclusively because he has been sentenced to deprivation of liberty.

Remuneration for prison work is essential for the reintegration of prisoners into society, as it ensures their livelihood and facilitates their reintegration. It is crucial that activities are aligned with the skills and abilities of the incarcerated person, promoting "their appreciation as a human being and the realization of their dignity," thus "enabling the incarcerated person to prepare for their future life outside the penitentiary establishment, as a citizen capable of collaborating with the society from which they were removed" (Cabral and Silva, 2010, pp. 160).

Bitencourt (2008, pp. 471) clarifies:

> By working, therefore, the prisoner participates in the economic and social development of the community in which he is inserted. Furthermore, "prison work is the best way to occupy the incarcerated person's idle time and reduce the criminogenic effects of imprisonment."

According to reports provided by former incarcerated persons during several meetings, it was found that the vast majority of individuals subject to the prison system show interest in work when offered the opportunity. Work activity is valued by them because it not only provides an alternative to the restrictions of the prison environment but also opens up possibilities for growth and social rehabilitation. Furthermore, it provides the incarcerated person with a way to occupy their time productively.

During one of the meetings, a former incarcerated person shared the following statement: "When they are not working, prisoners stay in their cells all day and only come out when it is time to sunbathe." This statement points to a reality where the lack of activities, whether related to work or study, results in a scenario in which prisoners have few alternatives beyond the walls of their cells while serving their sentences, generating idleness within the system. Such restrictions on sunbathing, which occur twice a week for two hours, further aggravate the feeling of confinement, negatively impacting the emotional and psychological well-being of incarcerated persons.

Work, in turn, is protected by a legal regime, not only through the LEP but also from the perspective of the Brazilian Constitution of

1988, which establishes work as a fundamental social right, thus reinforcing the notion of human dignity:

> Art. 6° The following are social rights: education, health, food, work, housing, transportation, leisure, security, social security, protection of motherhood and child-hood, and assistance to the destitute, in accordance with this Constitution. (Brasil, 1988).

Even so, it is evident from the reports and data presented that prisoners face a series of complex barriers within the prison system, and upon release, they encounter a landscape of freedom that does not offer concrete prospects for rehabilitation. For effective reintegration, a change in society's perspective regarding the rights and opportunities provided to individuals who have passed through the penitentiary system is essential.

Final considerations

By considering the perspectives of ex-prisoners, it is possible to understand the relevance of work as a fundamental tool for building a new life after serving one's sentence. However, it also becomes clear that there is a need to address the limitations and barriers faced by incarcerated persons in the prison system, which go beyond the issue of work. The lack of educational opportunities, the precarious conditions of detention, and the social stigma associated with incarceration are aspects that also influence the reintegration of incarcerated persons into society.

It is understood that "the resocialization of prisoners depends on the integration between work and the execution of the custodial sentence" (Cabral and Silva, 2010, pp. 167). Prison policies that aim to guarantee access to occupational and educational activities, in line with human rights and respect for the dignity of incarcerated individuals, are essential to providing a more humane experience and generating real opportunities for effective social reintegration after the period of imprisonment. In addition, actions in this regard can help promote self-esteem and build a more productive and healthy prison environment for all involved.

4
From FEBEM to Pedrinhas: Knowledge in crime

Alex Saraiva[10]

Bruna Maria Paixão Castelo Branco[11]

Alex's report

My name is Alex, and I lived a life of crime for twenty years. When I was twelve, I went to a breakdance club in Praça Deodoro, in the center of São Luís. There, I met a tough crowd. I studied at the old CEJOL, and they studied at Alberto Pinheiro. One day, in the middle of a drinking binge, they invited me to buy a Mazile[12] at the old Lusitana, a well-known place in the Praça Deodoro area. That's when a classmate stole a drink and a pack of cigarettes. The security guard at the place saw us, grabbed us, and took us to the Child Protection Council. There, they called our guardians. My father said he wouldn't go there. That's why I stayed at the Fundação Estadual para o Bem-Estar do Menor (FEBEM) for five days and then was released. Even after that, I didn't stop hanging out with the boys.

Then came the good times because the JEMs (Municipal Student Games) started, and the teacher invited me to be part of the soccer team. I even got into the swing of things and was playing really well. A scout saw me play and asked, "Who's the dark-skinned guy? Take him to the Sampaio tryout on that day!" So I went, and when I got there, he gave me a vest and said, "Do what I saw you do!" I humbly asked, "What did you see?" And he replied, "I saw how talented you are. With a lot of practice and discipline, you can become a professional." I was really excited! I passed the tryout and moved on.

One day, however, I found myself in a situation that would change my course. I was coming back from training when I saw a couple at the bus stop and thought, "There's going to be a party near my house." So I didn't think twice: I went and made the mistake. The next day, the coach called the team and the players to announce that we had qualified to play in the Copinha, a traditional soccer championship that takes place every year in São Paulo and is usually a showcase for new talent because it brings together teams from all over the country. We were very happy and continued to train with dedication.

However, two days before we were due to travel to São Paulo to play in the championship, the police arrested me. The reason? A gold chain and two cell phones. I was cut from the team and could not go to play in the Copinha in São Paulo.

The worst phase of my life came when I lost my mother. It was sad! She passed away in my arms, and I still remember her last words. My father quickly relapsed. He was already drinking; he was an alcoholic. And when my mother passed away, he gave in to drinking even more. A year later, I lost him, and this shook the family.

As time went by, these pains began to heal. I grew up and learned to get by, to work. I worked, but there were times when I wanted something more because that money wasn't enough. It's a shame that at that time I didn't know the meaning of the expression "a little with God is a lot, and a lot without God is nothing." So I continued to commit crimes, and before I knew it, I realized that I had already been talked about too much. Everyone in the neighborhood knew that I was involved in crime, and the rumors were circulating intensely. So I thought, "I'm going to move to another neighborhood; otherwise, I'll end up in jail or back in jail again."

I moved to my sister's house, where I spent thirteen years. During that time, I changed a lot, thank God! She and my brothers supported me a lot, even though I was in that situation. So, I came to Novo Horizonte, and it was the best choice I've made to date. It was there that God blessed me, and I met my partner, Cecília. Today, I live with her, and we're going to be together for six years. Not even prison made her leave me; when God brings people together, only He separates. That's my honesty—that's what we call each other.

Did you know that I once lived on the streets? I was a fugitive from the police, and they were looking for me for eight years. One day, I was sad and thought, "Wow, I'm doing everything wrong. I'm going to have to figure out how to get by." And that's when I decided to rob a gas station. I made a good amount of money at that time. With that money, I started dealing drugs and began making more money. I just showed off, wearing expensive clothes and everything that easy money gave me.

But easy come, easy go. The police started to surround me in every way. One time, I went out to play soccer. There were some houses on the edge of the field, and some street vendors came by and watched me. That was in the morning, around 8 a.m. Of course, I was suspicious, but I kept playing. In the afternoon, around 3 p.m., the police invaded the slum. The others and I managed to run, even under bullets. Luckily, we ran into the alley, and there was a patch of woods belonging to CAEMA (Environmental Sanitation Company of Maranhão, which owns some land in the city). We knew the entire trail through the woods because we were the ones who built it and walked there every day.

It wasn't long before I was arrested. When I got to jail, I went to my own place because I was very sad. It was only after two days that I started to socialize. Whenever possible, I played soccer to stop crying. I got sick, both psychologically and health-wise. Those were very difficult times. As the days went by, I started meeting people I already knew from the street. One time, I got into a fight with the general of the State, who lived in Coroadinho. He had been my friend since childhood, since the days of funk dances.

Since I already had some knowledge of prisons and prisoners—knowledge I had gained on the streets with them—they called me to the court to talk and asked if I wanted to join their team. Their argument was that, besides already knowing them, they had always respected me, and I had always respected them, ever since we were on the streets.

I thought, if I'm going to stay here for another four or five years, I'll at least try to work with the boys to improve our pavilion and the situation we were experiencing at that time due to the pandemic, with no visitors and all that. I said, "If it's up to me, we'll do it, on the same path." After five months of being in prison, I was invited to be a guard. I was responsible for receiving and transmitting messages (communications). Later, since I was the oldest in the cell at the time and already had some knowledge of discipline, of talking to troublemakers, and of communicating with the police, I also became a disciplina (a kind of leadership)in the cell. I tried to contribute to spending my time in prison in the best way possible. However, one time, I ended up arguing with a police officer and was subsequently punished.

Today, thank God, I have been released from prison, and with the support of my wife Cecília and out of love for her, I changed my life. I now live happily with her and bear the responsibility of a family man. I thank God for the opportunity He has given me. My family, whom I made cry so many times, is proud of the person I am today.

Discussion

The above narrative recounts the experience of a teenager from a low-income family in São Luís. The city has been the setting for his development and his relationship with violence and crime over the course of 20 years since the 1990s, despite encountering some opportunities along the way, such as becoming a soccer player for one of the most popular teams in Maranhão. Although it is a personal account, Alex's story reveals elements

characteristic of childhood and adolescence in vulnerable situations in Brazil, where there are few opportunities and possibilities
to change one's life, often leading to a new foray into the world
of crime.

In a parallel between reality and fiction, the story of São Luís
bears similarities to works such as *Captains of the Sands* (1988)
by Jorge Amado, which narrates this coming-of-age experience
on the streets, "living on the run from the police." It also shares
several similarities with a work released more than 40 years
after Amado's novel, this time on the big screen: *Pixote: a lei do
mais fraco* (*Pixote: The Law of the Weakest*). The film, released in
1980 and directed by Argentine filmmaker Hector Babenco, was
inspired by the book *Infância dos Mortos* (*Childhood of the Dead*),
published in 1977 by the Maranhão-born writer José Louzeiro.
This novel-reportage narrates the experiences of a group of
children and teenagers immersed in a world of violence, whose
survival is based on their relationships with characters in this scenario, such as drug traffickers and robbers.

The literary work was an adaptation of a report by Louzeiro,
who was working as a reporter for *Folha de S. Paulo*, covering
Operation Camanducaia. This operation took place in São Paulo
with the aim of removing children and teenagers from the
streets of that city and culminated in one of the bloodiest actions
that occurred in Brazil in the 1970s, involving the detention and
torture of 93 children and teenagers aged between 9 and 14. It
was dawn on October 19, 1973, when the victims were collected
from the streets and taken to the triage centers of the FEBEM
system in São Paulo. Many of them had no record of involvement
in crimes. From there, they were taken by bus to the side of the

Fernão Dias Highway, on the border with Minas Gerais. Of the 93 boys taken, 51 arrived in the city of Camanducaia, Minas Gerais, naked, scared, and hungry. Their arrival caught the attention of the residents and attracted media professionals. However, the remaining 41 boys never appeared. Frontana (1999, pp. 167) emphasizes that the state of nudity and the injuries the boys exhibited captured the attention of the city's residents, and only after their statements was it possible to understand what had happened.

These actions to curb marginalized children became a priority for the Military Dictatorship. The increase in poverty and the number of children on the streets created a sense of insecurity among the population, leading to measures aimed at reassuring the public. To address the situation of children and adolescents, the National Foundation for the Welfare of Minors (FUNABEM) was created in 1964, in accordance with Law No. 4,513 of December 1, 1964 (Brasil, 1964), replacing the Minors' Assistance Service (SAM).[13] As part of this new institution, the FEBEMs were created in 1967.

Teixeira (2012) highlights that Operation Camanducaia was one of the best-known social cleansing actions. However, this type of operation was recurrent in the 1970s. Aimed at curbing criminal actions in large urban centers, its main targets were marginalized children and adolescents.

> From that moment on, street *children* become more blatantly *street children* and as such the solution to the "problem" that they constitute must be sought not in the civilizing program of eradicating abandoned

children, but in the arena of open repression, in which other "problems" of disorder also manifest themselves. (Teixeira, 2012, pp. 174).

According to Schneider (2013), José Louzeiro was the first reporter to arrive in Minas Gerais, and the boys' testimonies were used in constructing the scenes narrated in the book *Infância dos Mortos*, reflecting the misadventures of the group led by Dito and their experiences on the streets and in correctional institutions. However, the details of Louzeiro's report did not have the impact he had planned upon arriving at the newsroom, which made the testimonies a reference for the literary work and, later, for the film that had a significant box office impact.

> I thought about becoming a writer thanks to the 1964 coup. I went to do a report (Folha de S. Paulo) about street children "thrown away" by the São Paulo police in the Minas Gerais municipality of Camanducaia . The censors reduced my article to about twenty lines. I left the newsroom, returned to Rio, and wrote the novel "Infância dos Mortos," from which the film "Pixote" was based. (Costa, 2005, pp. 155).

Pixote: a lei do mais fraco was released in 1980 and references the daily lives of marginalized children in the 1970s. Although the work is set in São Paulo and Rio de Janeiro, it shares much in common with the testimony of the teenager from São Luís.

The film depicts the daily lives of a group of children of different ages. Pixote, the youngest, is 10 years old, while Lilica is about to turn 18. With little education and fragile family ties, the group supports each other within the resocialization unit, needing to defend themselves against abuse and violence committed by staff and other incarcerated persons. Several scenes in the film depict physical violence explicitly committed by staff members of the units.

On the streets, they are vulnerable to drug dealers and pimps and are subject to various possibilities of being abused or becoming perpetrators of violence, whether by pickpocketing or assaulting people to commit petty crimes such as stealing purses, wallets, and necklaces. Even in such harsh realities, traces of the common discoveries of childhood and adolescence remain. Right at the beginning of the film, in the first scenes of the protagonist at FEBEM, a narrative unfolds that shows the boy witnessing sexual violence and, the next day, getting excited while watching a football match. Scenes also portray difficulties with literacy and the discovery of sexuality.

Marcello (2008) analyzes that the film oscillates between the violence present in scenes of marginality and characteristics of childhood, which are evident in the formation of children, mainly Pixote, the protagonist of the film.

> One of the most moving elements of the film *Pixote* is precisely the oscillation proposed by Babenco between the apparently genuine universe of the child and his immersion in the cruelest of worlds, that of the 'minors' in Brazil. As is the case of the first robbery carried out by the newly formed gang (Pixote, Dito, Lilica and Sueli), in the middle of the scene, the prostitute lures the client into an ambush, the three minors appear behind a curtain, ready to carry out the robbery. The tension caused by the *close-up* of the faces of the three, however, without failing to show the weapons that each one had in

their hands, is broken by Pixote's grimace , made as if he were just responding to a rudeness […]. (Marcello, 2008, pp. 116).

Just like in Alex's testimony, the ambitions of children are reflected in the boys portrayed in the film. Alex envisioned becoming a soccer player, but his involvement in crime obstructed his plans. In one of the scenes, Pixote expresses his intention to leave crime and become an artist when he turns 18, perhaps joining a band and achieving success. However, the relationships and contacts he makes on the streets lead him further into a marginalized reality. Without an education, far from his family, and a fugitive from a FEBEM unit, he becomes increasingly involved in crime, witnesses Dito and Chico die in violent acts, sees Lilica leave, and is thrown out of Sueli's house.

At the end of the film, alone and without friends or family, he balances on a train track as if seeking balance in life. It is unclear where he is going or whether his existence will endure; the ending is open, mirroring the uncertain existence of that boy in fiction.

The relationship between reality and fiction extends beyond the association of Alex's testimony with what is depicted on the screen. The film features a cast of mostly children and adolescents from socially vulnerable situations. To emphasize that the work represents a Brazilian reality, director Hector Babenco provides a prologue that highlights the scenario presented in the film. His introduction, transcribed in full, outlines the social context of the country during the film's production:

This is a neighborhood in São Paulo, a major industrial hub in Latin America that accounts for 60% or 70% of the country's Gross National Product. Brazil is a country with 120 million inhabitants, of which approximately 50% are under 21 years of age, of which approximately 28 million children live in conditions that fall below the standards required by the United Nations International Rights of the Child. There are also approximately 3 million children in this country who are homeless, who have no home and who have no defined family background. The situation for children is somewhat more chaotic when we consider that children are only liable to conviction for crimes committed after the age of 18, which allows some adults to entice children under 18 years of age to commit some type of crime or delinquency, knowing that they will not be punished. At most, they will be sent to a reformatory where they will spend a couple of months and, due to pressure and the lack of vacancies, they will be automatically released. This neighborhood, for example, is a neighborhood where families of workers from neighboring factories live, very large factories. The typical scenario is that the father and mother go to work and the children stay at home. The person who takes care of them is usually an older sister or a neighbor who is paid to do so. Fernando, for example, who is the main character in the film Pixote, lives with his mother and nine other siblings in this house. The entire film is played by children who belong to this social background. (Babenco; Louzeiro; Duran, 1979, verbal information).

During filming, the protagonist, Fernando Ramos, demonstrated that difficulties in teaching and learning could interfere with his career as an artist. In an interview with the documentary *Pixote – In Memoriam* (2007), casting director Fatima Toledo stated that the choice of actor Fernando Ramos to represent Pixote was made by director Hector Babenco because of the expressiveness in his gaze, despite his difficulty reading.

After the film's positive reception and sudden fame, Fernando Ramos believed he could pursue a career as an actor. He appeared in a few films and soap operas, but his struggle to memorize scripts due to his reading difficulties hindered his dream of becoming an artist. At home, one of his brothers was already involved in car thefts. Fernando also began committing robberies and getting involved with drugs, resulting in two arrests: once for stealing a television set and the second time for carrying a revolver. His arrests received extensive media coverage, with many associating him with the character in the highly successful film of his acting career.

Married and a father, Fernando was murdered by police on August 25, 1987, at the age of 19. He was chased by officers after being suspected of robbery. While fleeing, he managed to hide under a bed but was executed outside. This murder occurred four months after the death of his brother Paulo Ramos da Silva, who was shot in an unsolved crime. On April 4, 1990, Valdemar Ramos da Silva, another of Fernando's brothers, was found shot dead inside a Passat car. According to Louzeiro (1993, pp. 126), his death was attributed by police to Vitor José de Carvalho. Although he was in prison, he allegedly led a death squad called

"10 Justiceiros." He knew the victim because they had been cell-mates in one of Valdemar's prisons and claimed to be friends.

Far from fame, Fernando was murdered like Pixote's friends in the film he starred in. He was also pursued by the police, whose violent behavior is depicted in Hector Babenco's film. His adolescence and early adulthood carry the same uncertainties as the boy who says goodbye to the screen while balancing on train tracks, and they mirror those of Alex from the narrative that begins the text. Fernando learned to live on the run, discovering love and meeting Cida, the mother of his only daughter—a woman who was as much of a companion to him as Cecília is to Alex.

Conclusion

The story experienced by Alex and the representation of vulnerable children and adolescents presented in the film *Pixote: A Lei do Mais Fraco* (1980), despite their temporal and geographical differences, show similarities to a reality in Brazil, accentuated by public policies prior to the Statute of Children and Adolescents (ECA), whose purpose was to remove children and adolescents from the streets and incarcerate them in resocialization units. Although FUNABEM was created with the precepts of resocialization, providing opportunities for education, food, and leisure to contribute to resocialization away from crime, its advertising campaign portrayed the State as the guardian of these children (at the time, there was the expression "Children of the State"). In practice, however, it stripped away the family ties of these children; investments in education were weak, and violence was a crystallized practice within the institutions, orchestrated both among the incarcerated persons and by the employees of the units.

Physical, verbal, and sexual violence were among the reports of children and adolescents who survived Operation Camanducaia and are a snapshot of this invisible context in society. Whether on the run or released from the units, with a lack of education, all that is left is to dominate the streets. In both fiction and reality, reports of robberies, life on the run, living on the streets, and involvement in drug trafficking correspond to the daily lives of children and adolescents, whether they are from São Paulo, as portrayed in fiction, or from São Luís, as in the testimony presented. These stories are intertwined and constitute the memory of vulnerable childhood and adolescence in Brazil.

Today, after the Statute of Children and Adolescents has been consolidated, the country has emerged from a military dictatorship, and issues arising from violence are more widely debated in the media. Is it possible to say that this reality has truly changed? At the conclusion of the text and the theme, there is still no room for a definitive point.

5
Daily life in the São Luís women's prison unit

Lucia Santos Alves[14]

Yasmin de Sousa Andrade[15]

Introduction

In Brazil, there are more than 42,000 women in prison. This data was released by the *World Female Imprisonment List* in 2022, exposing a situation of hyper-incarceration, with Brazil ranking third internationally as the country that incarcerates the most women. In Maranhão, according to the consolidated report of the National Penal Information System (SISDEPEN) from December 2022, there are 478 women in a state of deprivation of liberty.

Research indicates that situations of vulnerability exist within women's prisons (Soares and Ilgenfritz, 2002). These vulnerabilities involve both the relationships between incarcerated persons and prison officers, as well as family relationships affected by the absence of family visits (Diniz, 2020; Braga and Angotti, 2019). The relationship between incarcerated persons and prison officers, especially disciplinary officers, tends to be quite repressive due to the existence of absences or PDIs (Internal Disciplinary Processes), which, as Diniz (2020, pp. 30) notes, follow "the classification of the law outside and the regulations inside," often resulting in the incarcerated person being unable to work or progress in the regime for up to a year.

Regarding family visits, research has shown them to be the main means of bringing food and hygiene products into prisons (Godoi, 2015). In women's prisons, the relationship between family members and incarcerated persons is shaped by social stigmas attributed to female prisoners, who are judged for not conforming to the "social standards of a fragile and docile woman" (Braga and Angotti, 2019, pp. 30). Given this situation, some prisons in the country hinder this relationship, for example, by scheduling family visits on weekdays, further restricting access for family members (Braga and Angotti, 2019).

Both laws, institutions, and prison policies are predominantly focused on the male figure and only adapted to meet female needs (Braga and Angotti, 2019). Women, in turn, have been defined by various criminological and penitentiary theories (Andrade, 2011), but they are rarely, if ever, heard. Fortunately, there are exceptions, such as the works of Diniz (2020); Soares and Ilgenfritz (2002); Braga and Angotti (2019); Padovanni (2018).

When women are heard, complaints about the lack of personal hygiene materials, space limitations, poor food quality, cell cleanliness, and the presence of rats and cockroaches at night are frequent (Soares and Ilgenfritz, 2002). In the Women's Prison Unit of São Luís-Maranhão, considered the best in Brazil according to the metrics of the former National Penitentiary Department (now the National Secretariat for Penal Policies), some of these problems persist. This is clearly reflected in Lúcia's account, below.

Lucia's story

I, Lúcia, was born in 1962 into a family in the countryside of Maranhão, raised by my parents, who always taught me and my siblings the difference between right and wrong, good and bad. We were brought up with these teachings, learning what we could and couldn't do. This guided my childhood, adolescence, and adult life, always striving to do my best and never taking what wasn't mine. At the age of 32, I started working in Palmas, Tocantins, for a federal company after passing the civil service exam. Since they needed employees, I was quickly called to work as a sales assistant and was soon promoted to manager. Everything was going well, but then my mother got sick, and I requested a transfer to Maranhão. However, since there were no vacancies in São Luís, I was assigned to work in the countryside.

I worked for several years until, one day in 2005, I received a telegram stating that I had been fired. They dismissed me for just cause, accusing me of embezzlement, claiming I had stolen from the company.

At that time, I was alone. My daughter was the person who could help me, but she was studying in Rio de Janeiro, and I preferred to keep everything that was happening to myself. I didn't tell anyone in my family, and I didn't even tell my daughter on the phone. Then, a friend found me crying in a square in São Luís and recommended a lawyer to help me. This lawyer, an elderly man, helped me, took me to do what I needed to do, and accompanied me everywhere. Sometimes he would call me from his office and invite me to go out, saying that we would go here and there, but I always refused. When I refused, he would say, "You were accused, you did it, and you will pay. You will go to jail." He was not a lawyer who gave me hope; he was always very harsh with his words. The office was in the city center, and I always left there hot-headed, crying, and desperate. And so, the years went by, and I was never arrested.

One day, my daughter moved to São Luís, and I told her everything that had happened. She then asked us to go to the lawyer's office, where he explained to both of us that nothing would happen, there was no evidence, and that was why the case had been archived. So we calmed down and moved on with our lives. My daughter married her husband, who had just arrived from another country, and then they had their first child, who is now 6 years old. We were happy at home; our family has always been happy. But one day, the federal police knocked on my door with an arrest warrant for me. That was on March 24, 2019, and it was a shock—first because we weren't expecting it, we didn't know there was a possibility the case would be reopened. But even though I was scared, I had to go. I got into the police car with all the neighbors watching me and went. They sent me to do the physical examination, and then I was taken to the women's prison.

There, they put me face down against the wall, standing for about 30–40 minutes, listening to the women who work there laughing and criticizing me because I was crying and saying I was innocent. They mocked me and said that was what everyone who went there said. When I was arrested, I found out that my lawyer had passed away and hadn't informed me that the case had been reopened. So my daughter hired a new lawyer, and he arrived at the prison after me. Then the officers criticized me because, according to them, I hadn't even arrived, and I already had a lawyer. They gave me clothes to change into, a pink set. I don't know if they still give out these sets today. Then they took me to a hallway with several small rooms on the right and left sides. I went to the right side because that was the side for the prisoners who hadn't been convicted yet.

I was always crying a lot; after all, I wasn't expecting that. They left me in a very cramped cell. The cells had 9 compartments, but it was always very cramped; sometimes, there were 12 of us, and some of us always slept on the floor. Since I have a problem staying in closed spaces, I became even more uncomfortable and started walking between one bed and another. Then a girl came and told me that if I didn't stop walking, she was going to kill me. The girls who were there were scared because she had already been arrested, and they knew the woman. So one of them said to me, "Look, ma'am, go over there to the door, and when someone passes by, tell them what she told you because this girl could kill you while you're sleeping." So I went to the door, and when one of the chiefs came, I called her. She opened the cell, asking what had happened, and I told her. Then she asked the others if what I had said was true, but everyone inside remained silent. I believe they were afraid of the woman. So the agent left and closed the cell again. I asked if I couldn't walk inside, and she said I could. So I continued, but the others all remained silent. After a while, they took the woman who threatened me away, and the atmosphere even improved.

I didn't sleep; I just cried. The food wasn't good, and I spent several months there on the right side. But I would go out of the cell to the court, and everyone respected me. I treated everyone well. We shared many experiences; we shared our pains, especially with the mothers who left their children outside. Since I have several health problems—diabetes, high blood pressure—and I always needed to visit the nurse, every time I went, it was the same thing. I would always go through the search. The prison guards would direct me to a room and search me. They would tell me to squat and cough. It was always the same thing, to enter and to leave the cells. My daughter always visited me on visiting days. She never missed a Sunday. She would bring me fruit and everything they allowed. It was always the same thing: I would leave the cell, go to the search room, undress, squat, and cough. When I returned to the cell, the same thing happened.

One day, they told me to go to the left side, the side where the condemned women were kept. They gave me a thin, dirty mattress, and I went. There were people of all ages there, some older women and some much younger than me. There were some cheeky ones, and with a lot of conversation, they would sometimes get better. At night, we would pray and watch TV because one of the incarcerated persons had a TV inside. One of them had a Bible, and I asked her to exchange her Bible for my fruit, and she gave it to me. I still have that Bible, and I always read it at home. At the back of our cell, there was a sewer gallery, and we could hear the rats all night long. The girls were able to lie down and sleep. They would lower the curtain and sleep. I was always walking around the cell a lot; I couldn't sleep well. I was always very breathless. Sometimes the officers would walk on the floor, on the upper part, to see if anything was wrong. But when they were downstairs, they would tell me to stop walking.

When they searched the cell, they went through everything and messed up our things. Before they opened the cell, we had to keep our heads down and sit on the floor, unable to look at them. Other times, they would take us in a line to the courtyard and go through everything in the cells to look for something illegal. It was very embarrassing. We couldn't look at anyone, we couldn't talk. When they found something, even drugs, things got much worse. We were all put in the courtyard and had to listen to a lot of things, things I never thought I would hear in my life.

And as I said, when we returned to the cell, everything was a mess. Some of the incarcerated persons were sent to a smaller room for several weeks, and sometimes even months, where they were subjected to internal disciplinary proceedings. They were left there alone, only receiving food and water. No one heard from them. Sometimes it was so bad that some of them took their own lives. We woke up and heard the news of two women who had hanged themselves with a bed sheet during the night. They couldn't handle the loneliness, the pressure, and especially the rejection. In addition to the internal disciplinary proceedings, we could also have our sentences increased if the officers found drugs or something prohibited inside the cell. If it was marijuana, it would be 2 or 3 years longer. Many of them were only there because of these punishments.

In terms of hygiene, the water bottles, for example, were dirty. Anyone could see that it wasn't right for anyone to drink water from them, but since there was no other way, we had to drink the water anyway. They also gave us a personal hygiene kit every month, which came with: four toilet paper packs, a toothpaste, a toothbrush, two small packages of washing powder, four bars of soap, two packages of sanitary pads, and a liter of bleach. And when the family brought bed linen and underwear, they called us and we signed to prove that we had received them. Sometimes I saw that the things my daughter sent were not what I received, but I also preferred not to say anything, for fear of what might happen, of how they might treat me if I said anything about the agents.

When there was a test, I took it. I took the ENEM test and got the necessary score. I was called by Pitágoras College, but I couldn't enroll because I had a problem with my completion certificate. There was a fire at the school where I did my third year and I was never able to solve the problem. But if I had been able to enroll, I would probably have graduated today. I heard that the girls who took it have already graduated. We also had some courses there, such as computing, sewing, baking, cake and savory snack making, hotel secretarial work, and a few others. I always asked to take them, but they wouldn't accept me. When I was almost ready to leave, I took the computing course and finished it quickly because I already knew a few things. I had worked with typing.

Later, I was assigned to sewing, but since I had a problem with my hand, I was diagnosed with carpal tunnel syndrome. My hand began to hurt, and they started listening to me complain about the pain. It ended up getting to the boss's ear, and they took me out of sewing. So I never left the cell again. I always stayed there. Some of them left and came back, did external work, or had some internal work. There were those who took courses, but others stayed too. When it was like that, we only left when we needed to do something outside the cell or when we had to sunbathe. I stayed there for many months without leaving. Then other courses appeared, and my name was put forward. There was also the Universal Church, which I went to a few times, but I was always denied permission to go to services. I didn't understand why, but I could only obey the order.

And the days went by. I was always going to the infirmary because of my illnesses, and there was a nurse there who was always very attentive to me, telling me to stop crying because my blood pressure wouldn't go down if I didn't stop crying. I also had a lot of trouble sleeping, and she prescribed me medicine for that. Before that, I couldn't sleep at all, and every time I had to leave the cell, I had to go through the inspection room and go through all that humiliation of having to squat and be searched. One day I was handcuffed and taken to the men's prison to do some tests that were available there but couldn't be done in the women's prison. And as always, I had to go through the search, always squatting, facing forward and backward. It was very difficult. It was the hardest year of my life. I never thought I would go through something like that, but if it was some sin I had to pay for, it's paid for.

One day I went to the boss's office. She asked my name, and I told her. She looked at my record and saw that I had been sentenced to 8 years in prison, so she started treating me with great disdain, throwing in my face all the years I had left, saying that I had only served one and still had a lot of prison time ahead of me, with great arrogance. But I told myself, deep down, that this was just punishment, so I went back to my cell, very dejected. My diabetes was very high, my blood pressure was high, my hair had turned very white, and there was no dye there. But thank God, everyone liked me. The girls there comforted me, and we cried together.

During the day, some girls cleaned the cell. Each one had their own day, and some were chosen to do the external cleaning. The sewage system had no drainage, so the incarcerated persons helped by sweeping it with brooms. We watched from the outside and smelled the stench. I don't know how the people who cleaned there didn't catch any bacteria. Sometimes some of them got sick. Once a week, I went to the gym and did my exercises so I wouldn't get out of breath, and then I actually got used to that place. My breathing started to improve. I started to feel better. I read the Bible and prayed a lot there. They asked me if I wanted to be baptized there, but I didn't want to. I promised myself that I would be baptized in a Universal Church when I got out, and I did.

My daughter tried very hard to get me out of there, mainly because of my poor health, but all her attempts were in vain, and the judge never approved it because, according to him, there was a doctor and medication for me there. But I still had the same health problems. Then the COVID-19 pandemic arrived, and that's when the new lawyer my daughter hired managed to get me out of there. At that time, my daughter had a baby in her arms and was depressed, needing me even more. Thank goodness she had a psychologist friend who helped her a lot. But thank God, I managed to get out. After 1 year and 6 days in there, I came home very thin and weak.

But the judge summoned me to put on the electronic ankle bracelet, and one day I was called to put it on. I had it on for 24 or 30 months; I don't remember exactly. And since I took it off, I've been going to sign in at the Monitoring Unit whenever they call me. Sometimes it's every month, sometimes it's every two months; it just depends on them. To this day, I suffer with this whole process, even more so because I'm innocent. I know I am, and I didn't use the supposed stolen money. Since everything happened, I haven't been able to work anymore, and my daughter has been supporting me. If it weren't for her, I don't know what would have become of me.

This process will only end in 2027, and as soon as I am one hundred percent free, I will leave Brazil to live with my daughter, who has helped me so much and continues to help me. She sold everything she had to pay for a new lawyer for me because my lawyer from the beginning passed away. I just ask God that the judge allows me to do this because I am alone in this city and I want to help my daughter and take care of my grandchildren.

6
Gender, prison, and torture: Beyond an androcentric perspective

Elane Cristina Xavier da Silva[16]

Monica Piccolo[17]

Leonardo Leal Chaves[18]

Introduction

According to Becker et al. (2016), data on female crime are scarce, and analyses are often permeated by stereotypes and notions of women's inferiority. As a result, crime is predominantly analyzed from a male perspective. This article challenges that viewpoint. Based on the account of a woman, Elane[19], who was brutally tortured at the time of her arrest, the aim is to shed light on the specificities of female incarceration in Brazil. This article, in conjunction with Elane's account, will address issues such as the growth of female incarceration, the presence of torture in Brazilian prisons, and the reforms needed to eliminate this practice, a harmful legacy of the Brazilian dictatorship.

Using data from Infopen (Brasil, 2014) as a reference, the growth of the female prison population has surpassed that of male incarceration. Although in absolute numbers there were 534,401 men and 37,380 women incarcerated, between 2000 and 2014, the female incarcerated population grew by 567%, while the male population grew by 220%. The exponential growth of women incarcerated, more than double that of men, requires that female incarceration assume a leading role in specialized analyses and begin to be investigated in its specificities.

In 2005, the estimated time of Elane's report, the Integrated Penitentiary Information System (InfoPen) published that in a state population of 5,651,475 inhabitants—2,812,681 men (49.76%) and 2,838,794 women (50.23%)—there were 995 men and 226 women in provisional custody. The prison population totaled 2,623 men and 22 women, of which 995 men and 3 women were in a closed regime. In the semi-open regime, 327 men and no women were reported; in the open regime, 154 men and again no women; and as for provisional prisoners, there were 1,043 men and 15 women. Among those detained by the Police/Federal Justice, there were 35 men and 4 women in the closed regime; 46 men and no women in provisional custody; and 23 men and no women in the semi-open regime.

According to data made available in the Maranhão Criminal Bulletin, published in 2022, the state's prison population totaled 11,730 prisoners in 2021, of which 470 were women, corresponding to 4% of the total. Thus, despite the touted improvement in prison conditions, Maranhão did not escape the national trend of exponential growth in the number of women deprived of liberty, rising from 22 to 470 in less than two decades (SEPLAN/ IMESC, 2022).

Returning to the data from 2005, the probable time of Elane's arrest, among the women deprived of liberty, seven were literate, six had incomplete elementary education, one had completed elementary education, two had incomplete high school education, and two had completed high school. The majority were sentenced to between four and eight years. Five were arrested for indecent assault, two for qualified homicide, two for simple homicide, four for forming a gang, as accused by Elane, nine for drug trafficking, and three for other crimes[20].

Despite the importance of quantifying the number of people deprived of their liberty in Brazil and Maranhão, these data do not account for the most striking element in Elane's account: the torture she endured at the time of her arrest.

Understanding the persistence of torture as a strategy for police officers to obtain information requires a closer look at Brazil's political transition after 21 years of civil-military dictatorship (1964–1985). This brings us to discussions in the field of Transitional Justice, which can be understood as a set of actions, devices, and studies that emerge to confront and overcome internal conflicts, systematic violations of human rights, and massive violence against social groups or individuals that occurred in a country's history. The main objective of Transitional Justice is to definitively end the authoritarian regime and solidify a mature democracy, in which broad protection of human rights is observed, and compliance with obligations defined by the international system is ensured. From these agreements, the following rights emerge: 1) the victim's right to see justice done, 2) the right to know the truth, 3) the right to monetary and other non-monetary forms of restitution, and 4) renewed, reorganized, and responsible institutions (Wojciechowski, 2013).

A central topic in analyzing how post-dictatorial societies view their past is the discussion of "Transitional Justice" in Brazil after 1964, which remains a recent topic. This perspective brings to light various social demands related to rebuilding the values of a rule of law in societies that have endured massive human rights violations (a core feature of dictatorial regimes) and navigating the transition process guided by the "delicate tension" between justice and peace (Moura, Zilli and Monteconrado, 2010). While Brazil's approach to Transitional Justice has not followed a single path, it is often described as "permeated by logical discontinuity" (Moura, Zilli and Monteconrado, 2010) in its efforts to achieve these rights, lagging behind other Latin American countries.

During Brazil's transition, if the opposition is primarily interested in ending the dictatorship, it is possible that retrospective policies will be avoided to avoid disrupting redemocratization negotiations (Brito et al., 2004). This is particularly true in situations where there is little social pressure in favor of these policies during the process.

Transitional Justice does not refer to a specialized form of justice, such as electoral or military justice. Instead, it encompasses a set of mechanisms, approaches, and strategies to address a historical legacy of human rights violations. These initiatives may include prosecuting criminals, establishing Truth Commissions, and conducting other forms of investigation into the past; efforts at reconciliation in fractured societies; developing reparation programs for those affected by violence and abuse; memory and remembrance initiatives centered on victims; and reforming a broad spectrum of abusive public institutions (Mezarobba, 2010).

Specifically regarding the Brazilian transition, Carlos Fico (2012) establishes that its fundamental features, although elements that would guarantee the exercise of citizenship are noted, are impunity and frustration caused by the "absence of judgment of the military and of rupture with the past that, so to speak, made the transition inconclusive, due to the conciliation of the political elites" (Fico, 2012, pp. 10). Precisely this inconclusive character would foster Transitional Justice initiatives.

The commitment and dedication to recording and clarifying the circumstances of these arbitrary acts are added to previous efforts to investigate, such as the Commission on the Dead and Disappeared, established in 1995, based on the "demand of the families of the politically dead and disappeared, in line with the historical demand of Brazilian society" (COMISSÃO NACIONAL DA VERDADE, 2014, pp. 20). The argument by groups within the Armed Forces that the investigation was an act of "revenge," illegal, or biased for focusing only on military actions, particularly regarding the work of the CNV and its final report, would be raised again to discredit its efforts. The idea of national conciliation, though framed differently than it was in 1979, would involve the acknowledgment of four key findings: (a) proof of serious human rights violations; (b) proof of the widespread and systematic nature of these violations; (c) the characterization of crimes against humanity; and (d) the persistence of serious human rights violations. To prevent the recurrence of these violations and promote the deepening of the democratic rule of law, the report lists 29 recommendations, including 17 institutional measures, eight normative reforms of constitutional and legal scope, and four that would ensure the continuation of CNV's actions and recommendations.

These recommendations, as highlighted in the final report, stemmed from demands by public bodies. Three directly addressed the issue of amnesty. Recommendation No. 2 suggests identifying the public agents responsible for serious human rights violations during the period under investigation, given the incompatibility between Brazilian law and the international legal system, as well as the "extension of amnesty to public agents responsible for illegal and arbitrary detentions, torture, executions, forced disappearances, and concealment of corpses" (COMISSÃO NACIONAL DA VERDADE, 2014, pp. 965). This aligns with support for institutions and the functioning of bodies that protect and promote human rights, as expressed in Recommendation No. 17, particularly the "recognition of existing bodies — the National Human Rights Council (CNDH), the Special Commission on Political Deaths and Disappearances (CEMDP), and the Amnesty Commission" (COMISSÃO NACIONAL DA VERDADE , 2014, pp. 970). Prioritizing the promotion of reforms in these bodies' regulatory frameworks and improving their operational conditions is key. Another important measure involves the creation of a permanent body comprising members of these entities to follow up on the actions and recommendations of the CNV (COMISSÃO NACIONAL DA VERDADE, 2014, pp. 973).

The final report of the National Truth Commission, delivered on December 10, 2014, to President Dilma Rousseff, reflects the inconclusive nature of its findings, as outlined in its list of measures and conclusions. Amid criticism from the Armed Forces, several entities that had long advocated for the investigation of the facts also expressed dissatisfaction with the findings of the CNV. The concept of national conciliation presented in the report does not include agents of repression, protected by the absence of punitive measures due to the limitations of the Commission's mandate, although the "report may support future legal actions" (Napolitano, 2014, pp. 332).

Thus, the tensions resulting from this attempt to "settle accounts with the past"—a common way of referring to mechanisms within the Transitional Justice framework—have been unfolding since the approval of the Amnesty Law, and echoes of this debate can be found in various mobilizations to review its complex scope/exclusion, reciprocity/restriction, and the effort to clarify events that occurred between 1946 and 1988. It is crucial to understand how the Brazilian dictatorial regime institutionalized its State of Exception after 1964, as well as its notion of amnesty, which involved a type of "commanded forgetting," conveniently safe for the military during the agreed political transition (Lemos, 2018).

In an article published on the Conectas Human Rights website (www.conectas.org) on May 18, 2023, several recommendations from the UN Committee Against Torture (CAT) for combating torture in Brazil are listed. In April, Brazil underwent an evaluation by CAT experts, a procedure that all signatory countries to the United

Nations Convention Against Torture must periodically undergo. Brazil's last review had been conducted 20 years prior due to the State's delay in submitting its reports. According to CAT's assessment, effectively combating torture in Brazil would require the demilitarization of the police, an end to the mass incarceration of black people, and the guarantee of legal abortion.

The report found that torture and related violations remain prevalent in many parts of Brazil, especially in prisons and peripheral urban and rural areas, with black people, quilombolas, indigenous people, women, and LGBTI+ individuals being the primary victims. The Committee requested that Brazil provide, by May 12, 2024, information on measures adopted in response to its recommendations, particularly on four points:

1. Adopt urgent measures to end the excessive use of force, especially lethal force, by law enforcement and military officers.
2. Continue efforts to eliminate overcrowding in all detention centers.
3. Fully align the juvenile justice system with international standards and promote alternatives to detention, ensuring that detention is used only as a last resort.
4. Establish a network of torture prevention mechanisms in all states and ensure that these bodies have adequate resources and independence.

According to the Committee's experts, Brazil must take urgent measures to end the use of excessive force, especially lethal force, by police and military authorities. In this context, the demilitarization of the police is an important action. The UN CAT

recommends that Brazil: use less-lethal weapons during policing activities, especially in areas with a large presence of civil-
ians; strengthen independent oversight mechanisms for public
security agents, ensuring that all complaints of excessive use of
force are investigated; and guarantee reparations to victims and
families in cases of violations. The report also highlights the need
for adequate training for police and prison forces, the implementation of torture prevention measures in places of detention, the
creation of independent monitoring mechanisms, and ensuring
that victims of torture have access to necessary legal and medical assistance (Committee Against Torture, 2023).

The content of the report makes it clear that one of the pillars
of Transitional Justice, the reform of institutions directly involved
in human rights violations, is still incomplete. Reinforcing the
need to review police actions, Elane's report, which begins by
stating that she was unaware of the explanatory elements of
police persecution and describes in detail the torture she was
subjected to in order to provide information—a practice repeatedly denounced by political prisoners during the civil-military
dictatorship—reinforces not only the recommendations of
Transitional Justice but also underscores the presence of authoritarian debris in twenty-first-century Brazil. It is up to the State to
act to hold accountable those who systematically violate human
rights.

When we look specifically at the conditions of women deprived
of liberty, we recall the research carried out by Heidi Ann Cerneka,
coordinator of the National Prison Ministry for women's issues,

who, when emphasizing the inadequacy of the prison system for women, states:

> (...) To the State and society, it seems that there are only 440,000 men and no women in the country's prisons. However, once a month, approximately 28,000 of these prisoners menstruate. Sometimes, some of them become pregnant, which greatly complicates things for the prison system, as there is a need for prenatal care, a safe delivery and escort in the hospital, as well as a clean and suitable place to care for their newborn. A policy is also needed to ensure that a nursing mother does not miss a court hearing just because she has to breastfeed her child. (Cerneka , 2009, pp. 62).

According to Mariana Lucena de Queiroz, although the issue of deprivation of liberty has been regulated by the UN since 1955, it was only in 2010 that the discussion around female specificities came to the fore through the United Nations Rules for the Treatment of Women Prisoners and Non-Custodial Measures for Women Offenders, popularized as the Bangkok Rules, as they were the result of a meeting of experts in that Thai city. The author highlighted its main points:

> The special vulnerability of female prisoners and their children; the specific needs of pregnant women and women who breastfeed in prison; special hygiene needs for women, such as sanitary pads; the issue of specific medical treatment for women and the right to doctor-patient confidentiality and privacy during consultations; prevention and treatment of HIV and other sexually transmitted diseases; the right to confidentiality

regarding one's sexual history; issues relating to under-age prisoners, such as ensuring them equal educational opportunities as male incarcerated persons in the same conditions; foreign prisoners and how to ensure their rights and contact with family members, especially children and other dependent children; prevention of torture and undignified treatment; guarantees of good infrastructure in environments of deprivation of liberty (Queiroz, 2015, pp. 10).

At the time of Elane's arrest and torture, the Bangkok Rules had not yet been systematized. However, the ongoing cases of torture in Brazilian prisons, and the 2023 UN report, lead us to believe that the country is still far from implementing them, even though Elane described going to prison as a relief from the torture she suffered at the time of her arrest.

Elane's report

I was with my boyfriend when the police caught us. He had already told me that they were after us, but I didn't understand—I didn't know what was happening.

We were taken to the robbery and theft unit and initially questioned about the robbery. First, they questioned me alone, and they were polite, but then the aggressions started. That day, my period began because I was beaten so badly. After that, they took me to investigate the robbery. We first passed through the neighborhood where my mother lived. When we got close, I looked at my sister and shouted from inside the plainclothes police car, "Bruna, ask Mom to come after me." But she didn't understand. To this day, she feels guilty about that. When we arrived at my mother's house, I called for help, but they attacked me again, putting my head between my legs and suffocating me.

We finally arrived at the place where I lived with my boyfriend. They started digging but didn't find anything. Then they started pushing and kicking me again, asking me where the money was, but I didn't know. When the police got tired of searching the land where the house was, they put me back in the car and drove through several neighborhoods in the city until we arrived at a deserted beach, which many say is a dumping ground. They took me to the seashore and started digging a hole. At that moment, I thought they were going to bury me, and I believed I would die there. They themselves had said they were going to bury me. I was terrified. But instead, they beat and kicked me. I thought they were going to rape me. When that didn't work, we returned to the police station.

When we got back, they put me in a room, sat me in a chair, and handcuffed me to the table. That was when I could rest and sleep. They caught me with my boyfriend at 5 p.m., and I think it was after 1 a.m. when we returned to the police station. Then they woke me up at 5 a.m. with a punch to the stomach. I saw a lot of activity; they had caught the rest of the people they were looking for. I noticed they had also taken my things from my mother's house. That's when she found out I was under arrest, but they wouldn't let her see me.

They put us all in the same room, and the interrogation began again. Since no one said anything, they went after us. I was still handcuffed, but now I was on the floor, with my wrist tied to a chair leg. They started hitting me with bottles filled with water.

When they got tired, they told me to stand up and put a bag over my head. The next thing I knew, I was on the floor, out of breath, having passed out. Then they sat me on the chair and put my hand on the table, sticking a needle between my nail and finger several times.

The assaults continued until the afternoon—around 3 p.m. That's when my mother finally managed to see me. I was weak and covered in blood, mainly due to my period the night before. But that didn't seem to matter to the police; they just wanted information. I never imagined that a simple piece of information my boyfriend had asked me about would lead to this.

When my mother arrived, I was able to eat and rest a little. As time passed and night fell, a new agent arrived. She seemed to feel sorry for me, seeing me sleeping sitting up. She gave me a moldy mattress, which caused itching and sores. But on that mattress, I could sleep a little better, despite the rats gnawing at my feet and the cockroaches crawling through my hair.

At dawn, I was woken up by more punches to the stomach, and another interrogation session—accompanied by aggression—began. This time, they had more information that they needed me to confirm, even though I had already said I knew nothing. Despite everything, that day was somewhat calmer because it was busier and the week had started. Additionally, my lawyer had arrived. He saw my condition and said he would call the Public Prosecutor's Office. But that made things worse. The police officer called me in and, when we were alone, threatened and beat me, accusing me of being a "hotshot" with influential protection.

My lawyer left me some snacks, but when I returned, everything was gone—not even water remained. They said I had to drink from the cistern. The interrogation continued with more threats and aggression. When they got tired, they left me alone, and I slept. That day, I didn't wake up to punches; it was more peaceful.

A friendly janitor at the station bought me a newspaper at my request. I wanted to know what was being said about us. That's when I realized the gravity of the situation. I already knew my boyfriend wasn't good, but now I was being framed as a gang member. My world fell apart. All I could do was cry because the police's threats about life in jail seemed mild compared to what I was going through.

In the end, I was arrested. When I arrived in jail, the girls welcomed me. They treated my wounds, fed me, and comforted me as much as they could. I was still weak and covered in injuries from the assaults and the mattress. Of course, I faced difficulties there, as everyone does, but it was nothing like the horrors the police had said I would face.

7

Convict criminology at Maranhão State University

Ester Ametista Marques Mendes[21]

The Brazilian prison system has faced numerous challenges related to high incarceration rates, and despite constant discussions on the subject, the situation of the prison population, especially women, tends to be neglected and forgotten. Several factors, such as overcrowding, lack of hygiene, and humiliation experienced inside and outside the system, hinder the resocialization process, violating the fundamental principles established in the Federal Constitution (Brasil, 1988), particularly the principle of human dignity, enshrined in Article 1, item III, as an intangible foundation with absolute effectiveness. Furthermore, Law No. 7,210/1984, known as the Penal Execution Law (LEP) (Brasil, 1984), is often disregarded. Article 1 of this law establishes penal execution with the aim of fulfilling the provisions of a sentence or criminal decision and providing conditions for the harmonious social integration of the convicted person and the internee.

The lack of visibility and recognition of women's specific needs within the prison system contributes to their demands and problems being neglected, reinforcing the perpetuation of inequalities and hindering the implementation of appropriate measures for their social reintegration. On the other hand, education is a powerful tool in the lives of prisoners, including women. Studies have shown that access to education within the prison system is associated with several benefits, such as reduced criminal recidivism, the development of skills and competencies for the job market, and the strengthening of self-esteem and the ability to make informed decisions.

However, despite the transformative potential of education, few initiatives are implemented to promote a more comprehensive and broad educational formation within prisons. Generally, educational programs are limited to technical courses, religious teachings, and manual work, failing to explore other possibilities of intellectual and cultural formation that could enrich the process of resocialization and social reintegration of incarcerated people. For this reason, the Outra Visão Project seeks to provide people who have left the system and are still serving their sentences—through open, semi-open, and conditional regimes—in partnership with the Integrated Center for Penal Alternatives and Social Inclusion (CIAPIS), contact with education as an alternative for an effective and permanent exit from the world of crime.

The procedures used were developed, inspired by the Convict Criminology movement, initially developed in the United States and later in England, with the aim of stimulating academic production on criminology by people who have experienced the prison system.

However, as we live in a different reality due to cultural, economic, and social differences, Prof. Dr Karina Biondi developed a method inspired by Convict Criminology, in partnership with the University of Westminster, in the United Kingdom, through the Making Links project, coordinated by professors Dr Sacha Darke and Dr Andreas Aresti (Darke and Aresti, 2016). The method developed in Brazil began with an extension action carried out by students of the Law and Social Sciences courses at the State University of Maranhão at APAC (Association for the Protection and Assistance of Convicts) in São Luís, MA (Biondi and Madeira, 2021).

> All students are able to formulate their opinions, making classes productive and the project only served to further strengthen and promote what they already know, inserting their knowledge into a more academic scheme, but in a way that understanding was accessible to all of them. (Biondi and Madeira, 2021, 168).

It is important to emphasize that some incarcerated persons had no formal education at all. However, in order to reduce the exclusion they already experience in many areas, no minimum requirements were imposed, allowing everyone to participate in the course. UEMA students (as they are called) were always available to help APAC students whenever needed. In a similar way, the method was applied at CIAPIS through the Social Office, making it possible for graduates to access the university, investing in and promoting personal development through education.

In the Brazilian context, although the country's legislation is expressly characterized by the humanization of the process of serving sentences through the LEP and the Constitution, what we commonly see (if we look carefully) is a reality that contradicts what is provided for in the law. Prisoners in Brazilian prisons, contrary to popular belief—mainly shaped by sensationalist news and experts who do not experience the inside of prison— are marked by the precarious reality of the system.

In this context, the "Outra Visão" project provided reports from former incarcerated persons who experienced prison conditions where the *comarcas* (as the beds inside the cells are called) were shared by up to three people. With cells originally designed to house nine individuals, in practice they can be occupied by up to 14 incarcerated persons. This condition directly affects the quality of life of prisoners, their physical and mental health, and makes the resocialization process even more difficult.

This situation is attributed to the steep rise in the number of peo- ple incarcerated and high rates of recidivism, theoretically asso- ciated with the growth of crime. However, activists question this interpretation, introducing the concept of the "prison-industrial complex," in which the search for profit, combined with racist ideologies, is seen as a determining factor in filling these prison spaces with a population largely identified as "criminal."

The idea was then fostered that the only way to protect soci- ety from criminals would be through harsh sentencing practices, leading to more people being sent to prison and consequently the need for more prisons to be built. The prisoners, who are mostly Black, are transformed into a source of profit, demon- strating that punishment favors companies that, in turn, have an interest in perpetuating prisons. In the case of the São Luís Penitentiary Complex—formerly Pedrinhas—there is a strong focus on manual labor among prisoners, both men and women, such as making clothes for the state through knitting mills or block factories, with little focus on intellectual development. It is worth noting that in Brazil—similar to many slave states—the prison population changed drastically after the abolition of slavery, becoming disproportionately composed of Black people.

During a dialogue in various meetings with former incarcerated persons, one student observed that, in addition to a considerably larger number of racialized people in prisons, there was also a small number of people from higher economic classes. He mentioned that the treatment of these individuals was often—if not the majority—different from those who already had a history of marginalization in the outskirts. In light of this comment, we can analyze the historical context of slavery in Brazil, its end, and the creation of the Penal Code of 1890 (Brasil, 1890), which criminalized vagrants, drunkards, beggars, and capoeira players, beginning a mass incarceration of Black people—a process that continues to this day.

Although Brazilian law provides for other forms of punishment besides imprisonment, the reality is that persistent overcrowding and the presence of unconvicted people awaiting trial inside prisons generate a "domino effect" of factors that compromise the experience of incarcerated persons, undermining the supposed resocializing function of the system. In this context, it is essential to analyze how overcrowding is driven, primarily by the large number of unconvicted people, and how this condition discriminatorily affects the lives of racialized individuals in the Brazilian prison system.

In Maranhão, according to the latest data published by the Court of Justice of the State of Maranhão, through the UMF (Monitoring and Inspection Unit of the Prison System), the incarceration rate has been increasing exponentially. In June 2023, the rate was 171.14 per 100,000 inhabitants, higher than the previous year's rate of 167.5 per 100,000 inhabitants (UMF, 2023b). Currently, of the 11,595 prisoners, 3,681 are provisionally incarcerated awaiting trial (UMF, 2023a).

It is important to emphasize that prison, as we know it today, was not the first and primary means of definitive punitive measure. According to Angela Davis (2003), it is a process that, over time and with the rise of capitalism and the establishment of new ideological conditions, solidified to the point that it is now ingrained in the collective subconscious as the supreme method of punishment. The author notes that this process materialized because it made sense at a certain moment in history, thus raising the question of a process that occurred under the perspectives and circumstances predominant in the eighteenth and nineteenth centuries.

This change in perception regarding prison as a punishment system occurred mainly after the shift in understanding of the individual, who came to be seen as a being with formal rights and freedoms. This process gained strength after the French and American Revolutions, which consecrated new ideals about human dignity and the protection of individual rights. However, it is important to highlight that, unfortunately, these transformations were not extended to women, directly affecting the imprisonment of female bodies, because the "public status of individuals holding rights was largely denied to women" (Davis, 2003).

Debates about society and its relationship with prison include issues such as individual evaluation processes within the system as a parameter to define a prisoner with good behavior, and the results of this movement of punishment through prison to transmit a greater sense of security to society by imprisoning "criminals" and making them available for such evaluation and regulation processes.

At various points during the course, former students questioned the treatment they received within the prison system, which often hindered the reintegration process of those who were detained. The abuse they suffered at the hands of prison guards, both physical and psychological, was raised. In relation to women, they highlighted their demands for basic needs, which were denied and often given as perks, such as sanitary pads, provided only once a month along with a basic hygiene kit, among many other situations mentioned.

There are also policies in the complex for the individual assessment of prisoners, which yield positive or negative results; in the latter case, punishment is given based on behavior and performance within the system. I would like to emphasize the constant reminders from the ex-prisoners involved in the activities, and their ongoing concern regarding these disciplinary processes to which they were subjected, the so-called PDIs (Internal Disciplinary Processes). In these, punishments ranged from warning notices to solitary confinement, where they could spend days, weeks, and even months alone and without the possibility of leaving, in conditions unfit for habitation, and in some cases, affecting the progression of their sentences.

As previously mentioned, during the meetings, students shared their stories. This sharing between UEMA students and former incarcerated persons—individuals who have experienced the Maranhão penitentiary system, both male and female—played a fundamental role in understanding prison reality. During these moments, diverse experiences were brought to light, covering topics such as living in cells, division of tasks, activities carried out, conflicts, family visit days, food conditions, treatment by prison officers, physical and psychological violence, torture, and the welcome from cellmates. The meetings provided a space for listening and dialogue, where stories could be shared and understood collectively. This exchange of experiences allowed for the development of a deeper understanding of life in the prison system, serving as a warning for situations that were previously ignored, especially due to the lack of direct experience with prison. Direct contact with the stories of people who have lived the prison reality fostered empathy and understanding among the students. This more humanized approach has helped break down stereotypes and prejudices about incarcerated persons, promoting a more holistic and compassionate view of those serving time.

This approach allowed for a deeper and more contextualized view of life inside prisons, raising awareness of neglected issues and contributing to the development of empathy and understanding. Through this exchange of experiences, it was possible to expand knowledge about the prison system, promoting a more sensitive and conscious approach to issues related to imprisonment and the reintegration of incarcerated persons. The inclusion of real-life stories and experiences in these debates is essential for the search for more humane and fair solutions for the prison system, allowing for critical reflection and the construction of more effective social reintegration policies.

8

Crossing borders: Exploring prison education projects in Convict Criminology in Brazil and the United Kingdom

Ella Walsh[22]

Katharina Ammerer[23]

Rochell Bonnick[24]

Introduction

In April 2023, a remarkable journey began when seven master's students in Criminology from the University of Westminster in England embarked on a unique field trip to South America. The first part of the trip took the students to the vibrant streets of São Luís, where they had a unique opportunity to witness firsthand the transformative power of Karina Biondi's university outreach project. During the trip, they also visited Dr Fernando Mendonça's programs, which are specifically designed for the rehabilitation and reintegration of prisoners in open, semi-open regimes, and on parole.

This chapter serves as an engaging narrative, capturing the profound reflections shared by three of these master's students. Their accounts of the trip illustrate the impact of sharing experiences with students participating in Outra Visão, an inspiring project developed by Karina to promote the transformative power of education for people deprived of liberty and to introduce the perspective and movement of Convict Criminology in Brazil. These stories highlight the importance of considering the lived experiences of prisoners as an invaluable source of insider knowledge. In addition, the reflections presented here encompass a comparative analysis, drawing parallels between the prison projects in the United Kingdom, in which these students were involved, and the Outra Visão program in Brazil. By examining how both projects align with the principles of Convict Criminology—namely by promoting mentorship for prisoners and ex-prisoners in higher education and fostering research activism to reform the prison system—the students offer profound insights into the convergence of aspirations across borders.

Prison-university Convict Criminology projects in the UK

In 2012, Dr Andreas Aresti and Dr Sacha Darke at the University of Westminster began developing Convict Criminology in the UK, drawing inspiration from the groundbreaking work of American scholars Jeffrey Ian Ross and Stephen Richards.

Since its inception in the 1990s, Convict Criminology has flourished as a perspective and movement, laying the foundations for transformative and radical change within the discipline of criminology. Over the past decade, the internationalization of Convict Criminology has seen it become a global activist research movement. Through their dedication to developing Convict Criminology in the UK, Dr Aresti and Dr Darke have successfully run higher education projects at HMP Pentonville, HMP Coldingley, and HMP Grendon. Students from the University of Westminster participate in these projects as 'outsiders', providing them with an excellent opportunity to learn alongside 'insiders' in these prisons (Aresti, Darke and Manlow, 2016).

This exceptional learning environment fostered knowledge exchange through a collaborative learning experience for both in-prison and outside students. By taking students beyond the confines of the classroom and into prison walls, these projects facilitated the breaking down of social barriers and stigmas. Through these experiences, negative perceptions about prisoners, often prevalent in both society and academia, have been changed.

Reflection on the visit to the Outra Visão project

Entering Brazilian prisons, we were struck by the cultural and contextual similarities and differences between the British prisons we visited and the people we met in prison. The composition of the prison population in both countries is strikingly similar, with the vast majority of prisoners being male, young, poor, and uneducated. This brought to mind the rising incarceration rates in both countries, which have resulted from discriminatory policies and policing that target this population, modelled on the mass incarceration system in the United States. The discriminatory nature of these policies is also reflected in the racial composition of the countries' prison populations. In our study group in the UK, only three people were white and British, with the remainder being of Black, Latin American, or Asian origin. The same is true in Karina's study group and in Brazilian prisons more generally, and we found this to be even more striking there than in the UK. We saw hundreds of Black and Latin American people in prison, but not a single white person.

Considering the impact that a lack of education has on people's risk of coming into contact with the criminal justice system (Martins et al., 2022), and the many barriers that people from lower socioeconomic classes face in accessing education in Brazil and the UK, the importance of education programmes in prisons in both countries becomes obvious. This is beneficial not only for students (both inside and outside prisons), but also for the discipline of criminology itself, as it becomes enriched with much-needed lived experience accounts—essentially reality checks for academics working in the field. However, it also serves as a reminder not to neglect the activist side of Convict Criminology and to try to counteract not only the discriminatory policies and policing practices that lead to the incarceration of a large proportion of a given demographic group but also the lack of access to equal opportunities for education and opportunities for this group.

One clear difference between people incarcerated in the UK and Brazil is the average level of education. Although there are prisoners with low levels of education and even some who are illiterate in the UK, many are at a sufficient level of education to attend university courses. However, access to this education is difficult and should always be demanded, given the clear advantages that a university degree brings to any prisoner, whether it be access to better jobs or a lower likelihood of reoffending. Our criminology course for incarcerated persons is not supported or funded by the state, and we often rely on the goodwill of the respective prisons to let us in. In Brazil, the illiteracy rate among prisoners is a staggering 8%, while 70% have not completed primary school and 92% have not completed secondary school (Quirino et al., 2020). This makes the pool from which to choose participants for a university-level course much smaller. However, in Brazil, we had the impression that prison education is much more encouraged, and access to courses, books, and teaching materials is much easier than in the United Kingdom.

It is also important to mention the different levels of poverty in the two countries. Prisoners in Brazil are more likely to come from extreme poverty and be released back into it, which may explain the low average level of education. This also makes their access to education and equal opportunities upon release even more important.

Finally, one of the biggest differences between the countries is the prison culture. While life in prison in the UK is more individualistic and solitary, in Brazilian prisons there is a culture of camaraderie and support among incarcerated persons. This likely has a positive effect on people's experiences of prison in general and their experiences of studying behind bars. Overall, we found the Brazilian prison education project to be incredible, important, and necessary. We were impressed by the positive energy and enthusiasm of the students and teachers, despite the challenging nature of the project.

In his 1967 article entitled *Whose Side Are We On*, Becker (1967) suggests that, as scientists, we must acknowledge the limitations of our studies and identify the boundaries where our findings can be safely applied. By doing so, we can meet the requirements of our field and ensure that our research is not misinterpreted or misused beyond its intended scope. During our visit to São Luís, we had the opportunity to learn about Karina's project, which showed intriguing similarities to the prison-university project on Convict Criminology that we are involved in, in the UK. Karina's initiative addresses the challenge of low educational and literacy rates in Brazil by partnering university students with people incarcerated in open conditions. This collaboration aims to improve literacy skills and promote dialogue. The project also provides training for people in open, semi-open, and conditional conditions, allowing them to share their experiences of Brazilian prisons in the public debate. This initiative prompts reflection on the role of prisons and prisoners, offering fresh perspectives within contemporary society and academia.

Similar to the UK prison-university partnership on Convict Criminology overseen by Sacha Darke and Andy Aresti, the aim is to bridge academia and the prison system, within the framework of critical criminology. This UK project promotes education through academic courses and lectures for university students both in and out of prison. The aim is to amplify the voices of those with lived prison experience, making them part of academic criminology and research activism. Supporting incarcerated and formerly incarcerated individuals in pursuing academic positions, such as completing their PhDs, is also a key aspect (Darke et al., 2020).

Similar to Westminster's projects, Karina's initiative, called "Another Vision," provides incarcerated individuals with access to criminal justice debates, fostering alternative discussions about crime, criminality, and punishment. The project embraces the Convict Criminology through ethnography and participatory action research, fostering collaboration between students and incarcerated peers. This approach anchors criminology in prison experiences. This first-hand experience showed me how these opportunities empower incarcerated individuals to explore their past and present lives with the guidance of UEMA students. The importance of this project becomes evident, given that many vulnerable members of the community, especially from marginalized groups facing socioeconomic challenges, end up incarcerated. The students in this project shared the struggles of personal growth within the criminal justice system, shedding light on the harsh realities within the Brazilian legal framework.

In São Luís, we also had the opportunity to visit CIAPIS— Integrated Center for Penal Alternatives and Social Inclusion, where we were able to observe the projects of Dr Fernando Mendonça, a criminal enforcement judge. The project combines two services and functions as a social center, offering prisoners, former prisoners, and their families several services, including, for example, legal counseling considering socioeconomic factors and job placement. It also provides monitoring to prevent domestic violence and support for victims—all under one roof. Involving family members in the sessions increases understanding of the experience of the incarcerated individual.

This holistic approach helps with reintegration into society, echoing integrated services in the UK and fostering a supportive community. While social services and probation officers typically manage reintegration programs in the UK, Dr Fernando Mendonça's initiative emphasizes reintegration into society, addressing the disproportionate impact on marginalized groups in the penal system. Similarly, the UK could enhance its reintegration efforts by incorporating higher education into its plans, similar to Dr Fernando's model. The unity and safety observed between staff and incarcerated individuals during our visit left a strong impression, reflecting the sense of safety when interacting with incarcerated students in the UK.

Karina's project and Dr Fernando Mendonça's initiative serve individuals in open and semi-open conditions, whereas in the UK there is insufficient support after release, leading to less effective reintegration efforts. However, having a political figure like Dr Fernando helps solidify such movements seen in São Luís, perhaps a figure we lack in the UK. The transparent and impactful initiatives have inspired a greater commitment to research activism, employing principles of Convict Criminology that aim to enrich the criminal justice system by demystifying prisons through first-hand experiences.

Final notes

The journey undertaken by seven Master's Criminology students from the University of Westminster to South America was truly transformative. The stories and reflections shared by these students in this excerpt aim to provide valuable insights into the power of education in the rehabilitation and reintegration of prisoners, as well as the importance of the principles of Convict Criminology in promoting positive change in the criminal justice system worldwide.

The students' experiences in São Luís highlighted the parallels between the UK's Convict Criminology projects and Karina Biondi's Outra Visão initiative. Both projects share the goal of breaking down social barriers and the stigma associated with prisoners through education and knowledge exchange. It became clear that considering the lived experiences of prisoners is a valuable source of insider knowledge, providing a reality check for academics working in the field of criminology. As the students returned to the UK, they carried with them the understanding that their dedication to Convict Criminology can lead to positive impacts within their communities and the wider criminal justice system. This field trip serves as a reminder that promoting education and inclusion is vital not only for the rehabilitation of prisoners but also for the advancement of the discipline of criminology itself. By working collectively across borders and cultures, we can strive to create a more just and inclusive society for all.

Suggested projects, assignments or discussion questions

1. Research the living conditions in prisons in your city/region and compare them with those described in the book. What are the differences? How are they similar?

2. While reading the chapters, did you identify any situations that violate international human rights treaties? Which one(s)? Why?

3. Do you believe that the prison system and incarceration policies, as described in the chapters, are effective in promoting peace?

4. How do accounts from people who have experienced prisons differ from more conventional academic/scientific writings?

Notes

Presentation

1. Chief judge of the 2nd Criminal Executions, Sentences and Alternative Measures Court of São Luís.

2. Convict Criminology is an academic movement led by former prisoners and a critical perspective that argues that prisoners and former prisoners should participate in the production of knowledge about prison.

Introduction

3. Professor of the Department of Sciences University Social State of Maranhão. Research productivity scholarship holder from the National Research Council (CNPq), level 2.

4. Undergraduate in Nursing at Anhanguera College, popular educator and supervisor of the Outra Visão Project.

5. Undergraduate in Veterinary Medicine at the State University of Maranhão.

6. Criminology student of the Another Vision Project, at the State University of Maranhão.

7. Professor at the Department of Social Sciences at the State University of Maranhão.

8. Criminology student of the Another Vision Project, at the State University of Maranhão.

9. Undergraduate in Law at the State University of Maranhão.

10. Criminology student of the Another Vision Project, at the State University of Maranhão.

11. PhD student in the Postgraduate Program in History at the State University of Maranhão.

12. Popular alcoholic drink in the region at the time.

13. Law No. 4,513 of December 1, 1964 – Authorizes the Executive Branch to create the National Foundation for the Welfare of Minors, incorporating into it the assets and attributions of the Minors Assistance Service, and provides other measures. Available at: <www.planalto.gov.br/ccivil_03/leis/1950-1969/L4513.htm>. Accessed on: January 21, 2020.

14. Criminology student of the Another Vision Project, at the State University of Maranhão.

15. Undergraduate student in Social Sciences at the State University of Maranhão.

16. Criminology student of the Another Vision Project, at the State University of Maranhão.

17. Professor in the History Department of the State University of Maranhão. Research productivity scholarship holder from the National Research Council (CNPq), level 2.

18. PhD candidate at the Center for Interdisciplinary Studies of the 20th Century, University of Coimbra.

19. For security reasons, I did not have access to more specific information about the author of the report, such as the exact date of her arrest. I can only inform you that the event narrated occurred in the city of São Luís, Maranhão, in the mid-2000s .

20. I would like to point out that there seems to be some inconsistency in the data in the Report. In the composition of the prison population, there are 22 women. In the field of crime typology, there are 25. This fact can be explained by the lack of information provided by prison establishments.

21. Undergraduate in Law at the State University of Maranhão.

22. Masters student in Criminology at the University of Westminster.

23. Masters student in Criminology at the University of Westminster.

24. Masters in Criminology at the University of Westminster

References

Alvim, R. C. M. (1991). *O trabalho penitenciário e os direitos sociais*. São Paulo: Atlas.

Amado, J. (1988). *Captains of the sands*. Translated by Gregory Rabassa. New York: Avon.

Andrade, B. S. A. B. (2011). *Entre as leis da ciência, do estado e de Deus: O surgimento dos presídios no Brasil*. Master in Social Anthropology, Universidade de São Paulo.

Aresti, A., Darke, S. and Ross, J. I. (2023). Against bifurcation: why it's in the best interests of convict criminology to be international in scope and not a collection of individual country level organisations. *Justice, Power and Resistance*, 6(2), pp. 1–16.

Aresti, D. A., Darke, D. S. and Manlow, D. (2016). Giving Public Voice to Prisoners and Former Prisoners through Research Activism. *Prision Service Journal*, 224, pp. 3–13.

Barrouin, N., Portella, B., Vieira, E., Pereira, I., Cavalcante, J. and Oliveira P. eds. (2021). *Covid nas prisões: pandemia e luta por justiça no Brasil (2020–2021)*. Rio de Janeiro: Instituto de Estudos da Religião.

Becker, H. S. (1967). Whose side are we on? *Social problems*, 4(3), pp. 239–247.

Behan, C. (2014) Learning to escape: Prison education, rehabilitation and the potential for transformation. *Journal of Prison Education and Reentry*, 1(1), pp. 20–31.

Becker, A., Spessote, D. V., Sardinha, L. da S., Santos, L. G. de M., Chaves, N. N. and Bicalho, P. P. G. (2016). O cárcere e o abandono: prisão, penalização e relações de gênero. *Revista Psicologia, Diversidade e Saúde*, 5(2), pp. 141–154.

Biondi, K., Madeira, T. de J. (2021). Outra visão: novas perspectivas sobre o (e a partir do) sistema prisional. *Extramuros: revista de extensão da UNIVASF*, 3(1), pp. 151–170.

Biondi, K. (2022). Efeitos de alguns afetos religiosos: revoluções. In: A. Jarrin, B. Junge, S. T. Mitchell, L. Cantero and K. Biondi, eds., *Democracia precária: etnografias de esperança, desespero e resistência no Brasil*. Porto Alegre: Zouk Editora, pp. 171–190.

Biondi, K. (2016). *Sharing This Walk: An Ethnography of Prison Life and the PCC in Brazil*. Edited and translated by John F. Collins. University of North Carolina Press.

Birman, P. (2012). O poder da fé, o milagre do poder: mediadores evangélicos e deslocamento de fronteiras sociais. *Horizontes antropológicos*. v. 18, n. 37, pp. 133–153.

Bitencourt, C. R. (2008). *Tratado de Direito Penal*. 13th ed. São Paulo: Saraiva.

Bixio, B., Mercado, P. and Timmerman, F. eds. (2016). *Sentidos políticos de la universidad en la cárcel. Fragmentos teóricos y experiencias*. Córdoba: Universidad Nacional de Córdoba.

Braga, G. and Angotti, B. (2019). *Dar à Luz na Sombra: exercício da maternidade na prisão*. São Paulo: Editora Unesp digital.

Brasil. (1988). *Constituição da República Federativa do Brasil*. Brasília, DF: Presidência da República.

Brasil. (1890). *Decreto nº 847, de 11 de outubro de 1890.* Promulga o código penal. Available at: https://www.planalto.gov.br/ccivil_03/decreto/1851-1899/d847.htm. Accessed 29 July 2023.

Brasil. (2022). *Lei no 14.326, de 12 de abril de 2022. Altera a Lei nº 7.210, de 11 de julho de 1984 (Lei de Execução Penal), para assegurar à mulher presa gestante ou puérpera tratamento humanitário antes e durante o trabalho de parto e no período de puerpério, bem como assistência integral à sua saúde e à do recém-nascido.* Brasília, DF: Presidência da República.

Brasil. (1984). *Lei N° 7.210, de 11 de julho de 1984. Dispõe sobre a Lei de Execução Penal.* Brasília, DF: Diário Oficial da União.

Brasil. (1964). *Lei nº 4.513, de 1 de dezembro de 1964. Autoriza o Poder Executivo a criar a Fundação Nacional do Bem-Estar do Menor, a ela incorporando o patrimônio e as atribuições do Serviço de Assistência a Menores, e dá outras providências.* Brasília, DF: Presidência da República.

Brasil. (2014). *Infopen, Informações. Execução Penal.* Sistema Prisional, InfoPen–Estatística . Brasília, DF: Ministério da Justiça e Cidadania.

Brito, A. B., González-Enríquez, C. and Fernández, P. A. eds. (2004). *Política da memória: verdade e justiça na transição para a democracia.* Lisboa: Imprensa de Ciências Sociais.

Cabral, L. R. and Silva, J. L. (2010). O trabalho penitenciário e a ressocialização do preso no Brasil. *Revista do Centro Acadêmico Afonso Pena*, 13(1).

Cerneka, H. A. (2009). Homens que menstruam: Considerações acerca do sistema prisional às especificidades da mulher. *Veredas do Direito*, 6(11), pp. 61–78.

COMISSÃO NACIONAL DA VERDADE. (2014). *Relatório final.* Brasília: CNV.

COMMITTEE AGAINST TORTURE – UNITED NATIONS. Concluding observations on the second periodic report of Brazil. Genebra: United Nations, 12 jun. 2023. Available at: https://docs.un.org/en/CAT/C/BRA/CO/2. Accessed 9 February 2025.

CONSELHO FEDERAL DE MEDICINA – CFM. (2020). *Brasil gasta R$ 3,83 ao dia com a saúde de cada habitante.* Available at: https://portal.cfm.org.br/noticias/brasil-gasta-r-383-ao-dia-com-a-saude-de-cada-habitante-2/. Accessed 28 July 2023.

Costa, C. (2005). *Pena de Aluguel: escritores jornalistas no Brasil 1904–2004.* São Paulo: Companhia das Letras.

Darke, S. and Aresti, A. (2016). Connecting prisons and universities through higher education. *Prison Service Journal*, 266, pp. 26–32.

Darke, S., Aresti, A., Faisal, A. B. and Ellis, N. (2020). Prisoner-University Partnerships at Westminster. In: S. S. Shecaira, L. G. B. Ferrarini and J. M. Almeida, eds. *Criminologia: Estudos em homenagem ao Professor Alvino Augusto de Sá*. Belo Horizonte: D'Plácido.

Davis, A. (2003). *Are prisons obsolete?* New York: Seven Stories Press.

DEPARTAMENTO PENITENCIÁRIO NACIONAL – DEPEN. (2020). *Medidas de combate ao COVID-19*. Available at: https://app.powe rbi.com/view?r=eyJrIjoiYThhMjk5YjgtZWQwYS00ODlkLTg4NDg-tZTFhMTgzYmQ2MGVIiwidCI6ImViMDkwNDIwLTQ0NGMtND-NmNy05MWYyLTRiOGRhNmJmZThlMSJ9. Accessed 3 July 2023.

Dias, C. C. N. (2008). *A igreja como refúgio e a Bíblia como esconderijo: religião e violência na prisão*. São Paulo: Humanitas.

Diniz, D. (2020). *CADEIA: Relatos sobre mulheres*. Rio de Janeiro: Civilização Brasileira.

Earle, R. (2016). *Convict Criminology: Inside and Out*. Policy Press: Bristol.

Ferreira, A. P., Silva, P. M. C. A. and Godinho, M. R. (2020). Adversidades e Desafios do Sistema Prisional: uma revisão sistemática sobre a saúde penitenciária. *Revista de Medicina e Saúde de Brasília*, 2(9), pp. 270–286.

Fico, Carlos. Brasil: a transição inconclusa. (2012). In: C. Fico, M. P. Araujo and M. Grin, eds. *Violência na História: memória, trauma e reparação*. Rio de Janeiro: Ponteio, pp. 25–38.

Foucault, M. (1977). *Discipline and Punish: The Birth of the Prison*. New York: Vintage Books.

Frontana, I. C. R. da C. (1999). *Crianças e adolescentes nas ruas de São Paulo*. São Paulo: Edições Loyola.

Garcia, L. P. C. (2021). *APAC e religião: há eficácia de princípios cristãos no processo de ressocializacão de detentos?* Undergraduation in Social Science, Universidade Estadual do Maranhão.

Godoi, R. (2015). Vasos Comunicantes, Fluxos Penitenciários: entre dentro e fora das prisões de São Paulo. *Vivência: Revista de Antropologia*, 1(46), pp. 131–142.

Gutierrez, M. ed. (2012). *Lápices o rejas: pensar la actualidad del derecho a la educación en contextos de encierro.* Buenos Aires: Del Puerto.

Hughes, E. (2009). Thinking inside the box: Prisoner education, learning identities, and the possibility for change. In: B. M. Veysey, J. Christian and D. J. Martinez, eds., *How Offenders Transform their Lives.* Cullompton: Willan.

INSTITUTO DE PESQUISA ECONÔMICA APLICADA – IPEA. (2015) *Reincidência Criminal no Brasil: Relatório de Pesquisa.* Rio de Janeiro: IPEA.

Latour, B. (2005). *Reassembling the Social: An Introduction to Actor-Network-Theory.* Oxford: Oxford University Press.

Lemos, R. (2018). *Ditadura, anistia e transição política no Brasil (1964–1979).* Rio de Janeiro: Consequência.

Lins, P., Silva, M. de L. da. (1989). Bandidos e evangélicos: extremos que se tocam. *Religião e Sociedade*, 15(1), pp. 166–173.

Louzeiro, J. (1993). *Pixote: a lei do mais forte.* Rio de Janeiro: Editora Civilização Brasileira S/A.

Machado, C. B. (2014). Pentecostalismo e o sofrimento do (ex-) bandido: testemunhos, mediações, modos de subjetivação e projetos de cidadania nas periferias. *Horizontes Antropológicos*, 20, pp. 153–180.

Magalhães, F. L. (2020). *Projeto Outra Visão: O documentário.* [video] Available at https://www.youtube.com/watch?v=WRz3M-LuSBE. Accessed 28 Oct 2024.

Marcello, F. de A. (2008). *Criança e imagem no olhar sem corpo do cinema*. 2008. Doctorate in Education, Universidade Federal do Rio Grande do Sul.

Marques, V. A. (2015). *Fé & Crime: Evangélicos e PCC nas periferias de São Paulo*. São Paulo: Fonte Editorial.

Martins, R. C., Gonçalves, H., Blumenberg, C., Könsgen, B., Houvèssou G. M., Carone, C., Gil, J. D., Lautenschläger, P., Wehrmeister, F. C., Menezes, A. M. B. and Murray, J. (2022). School performance and Young Adult Crime in a Brazilian birth cohort. *Journal of Developmental and Life-Course Criminology*, 8(4), pp. 647–668.

Medrado, L. (2016). *Cristianismo e criminalidade: a adesão de bandidos ao Universo Cristão Pentecostal*. São Paulo: Fonte editorial.

Mezarobba, G. (2010). O processo de acerto de contas e a lógica do arbítrio. In: E. Teles and Vladimir Safatle, eds., *O que resta da ditadura: a exceção brasileira*. São Paulo: Boitempo, pp. 109–122.

Ministério da Saúde. (2003). *Portaria Interministerial nº 1.777, de 09 de setembro de 2003*. Aprova o Plano Nacional de Saúde no Sistema Penitenciário. Brasília, DF: Ministério da Saúde.

Morin, E. M. (2001). Os sentidos do trabalho. *Revista de Administração de Empresas*, 41(3), pp. 8–19.

Moura, M. T. R. de A., Zilli, M. and Monteconrado, F. G. (2010). A Justiça De Transição No Brasil – Um Caminho A Percorrer. In: K. Ambos, M. Zilli, M. T. R. de A. Moura and F. G. Monteconrado, eds., *Anistia, justiça e impunidade: reflexões sobre a justiça de transição no Brasil*. Belo Horizonte: Fórum.

Napolitano, M. (2014). *1964: A história do Regime Militar brasileiro*. São Paulo, Editora Contexto.

Padovanni, N. C. (2018). *Sobre casos e Casamentos: Afetos e amores, através das penitenciárias femininas de São Paulo e Barcelona*. São Paulo: Edfscar.

Paixão, E. B., Maia, R. and Cruz, M. (2021). Grito contra o genocídio nas prisões ecoa na ONU e na OEA. In: N. Barrouin, B, Portella, E. Vieira, I. Pereira, J. Cavalcante and P. Oliveira, eds. *Covid nas prisões: pandemia e luta por justiça no Brasil (2020–2021)*. Rio de Janeiro: Instituto de Estudos da Religião.

Parchuc, J. P. (2015). La universidad en la cárcel: teorías, debates, acciones. *Redes de extensión*, 1, pp. 18–36.

Piché, J. (2008). Barriers to studying inside: Education in prisons and education on prisons. *Journal of Prisoners on Prisons*, 1(17), pp. 4–17.

Pixote – In Memoriam. (2007). [Video] Brazil: Felipe Briso, Gilberto Topczewski.

Pixote, a lei do mais fraco. (1980). [Video] Brazil: Embrafilme.

Prando, C. and Godoi, R. (2020). A gestão dos dados sobre a pandemia nas prisões: Uma comparação entre as práticas de ocultamento das secretarias de administração prisional do RJ e DF. *Dilema: Revista de Estudos de Conflitos e Controle Social- Reflexões na Pandemia*, pp. 1–15.

Queiroz, M. L. de. (2015). A Abordagem Feminista das Relações Internacionais e Violações de Direitos Humanos no Brasil – Uma Discussão Sobre o Sistema Prisional. *Revista Transgressões Ciências Criminais em Debate*, 3(2), pp. 5–31.

Quirino Filho, J. D., Rolim Neto, M. L. and Nascimento, V. B. (2020). Incarcerated people in prisons: A public health priority in resource-poor settings. *Forensic Science International: Mind and Law*, 1(2).

Ribeiro, C. S. (2014). Do Direito Fundamental ao Trabalho, da Remição e da possibilidade de remissão em Execução Penal. *Revista Justiça do Direito*, 28(1), pp. 216–239.

Ross, J. I. and Copes, H. (2022). Convict criminology from here to there: a content analysis of scholarship in a growing subfield.

Criminal Justice Studies: A Critical Journal of Crime, Law and Society, 35(4), pp. 442–457.

Ross, J. I. and Vianello, F. A. (2021). *Convict Criminology for the future.* New York: Routledge.

Sánchez, A., Leal, M. C. and Larouzé, B. (2016). Realidade e desafios da saúde nas prisões. *Revista Ciência e Saúde Coletiva,* 21(7).

Santos, M., Salsamendi, E. S., Sánchez, A. and Larouzé, B. (2020). Arquitetura prisional e saúde em tempos de COVID-19: o uso de contêiners se justifica? *Informe ENSP.*

Schneider, S. (2013). *Ficções sujas: por uma poética no romance-reportagem.* Doctorate in Literature, Pontifícia Universidade Católica do Rio Grande do Sul.

SECRETARIA NACIONAL DE POLÍTICAS PENAIS – SENAPPEN (2024). Levantamento Nacional de Informações Penitenciárias. Brasília: Ministério da Justiça e Segurança Pública.

SEPLAN/IMESC. (2022). *Boletim Criminal do Maranhão – Sistema Penitenciário,* 3(3).

Soares, B. M. and Ilgenfritz, I. (2002). *PRISIONEIRA: Vida e Violência atrás das Grades.* Rio de Janeiro: Garamond Universitária.

Strathern, M. (1988). *The gender of the gift: Problems with Women and Problems with Society in Melanesia.* Berkeley and Los Angeles: University of California Press.

Teixeira, A. (2012). *Construir a delinquência, articular a criminalidade: um estudo sobre a gestão dos ilegalismos na cidade de São Paulo.* 2012. Doctorate in Sociology, Universidade de São Paulo.

UNIDADE DE MONITORAMENTO DO SISTEMA CARCERÁRIO – UMF. (2020). *Relatório mulheres presas.* Available at: https://novo gerenciador.tjma.jus.br/storage/portalweb/24_relatorio_umf_ mulheres_presas_mar_2020_18052020_1438.pdf. Accessed 15 July 2023.

UNIDADE DE MONITORAMENTO DO SISTEMA CARCERÁRIO – UMF. (2023a). *Relatório das Unidades Prisionais e Delegacias*. Available at: https://novogerenciador.tjma.jus.br/storage/arquivos/pris oes/78_relatorio_umf_dados_dos_presos_jun_2023_26_07_20 23_15_11_01.pdf. Accessed 3 August 2023.

UNIDADE DE MONITORAMENTO DO SISTEMA CARCERÁRIO – UMF. (2023b) *Taxa de Encarceramento: janeiro de 2022 a junho de 2023*. Available at: https://novogerenciador.tjma.jus.br/storage/ arquivos/prisoes/taxa_de_encarceramento_junho_2023_31_0 7_2023_15_37_37.pdf. Accessed 3 August 2023.

UNITED NATIONS. (2015) *United Nations Standard Minimum Rules for the Treatment of Prisoners* (the Nelson Mandela Rules), Resolution A/RES/70/175.

Viana, A. L. P. (2020). Como não confiam na gente e, ainda assim, entregam as chaves da nossa cela? Reflexões sobre autogestão prisional. *Novos Debates*, 6(1–2).

Vieira, G. R. and Stadtlober, C. S. (2020). O Trabalho no Cárcere Feminino. *Revista Prâksis*, 1, pp. 77–101.

Vital, C. (2015). *Oração de traficante*. Rio de Janeiro: Garamond.

Wojciechowski, P. B. (2013). *Leis de Anistia e o sistema internacional de proteção dos direitos humanos: estudo comparativo Brasil, Argentina e Chile*. Curitiba: Juruá.

Index

www.ingramcontent.com/pod-product-compliance
Lightning Source LLC
Chambersburg PA
CBHW070346270326
41926CB00017B/4005